User Guide

Institute of Management and Open Learning Programme

Series editor: Gareth Lewis
Author: Jeremy Kourdi

the Institute of Management
FOUNDATION

**Pergamon
Open
Learning**

Pergamon Open Learning
An imprint of Butterworth-Heinemann
Linacre House, Jordan Hill, Oxford OX2 8DP
A division of Reed Educational and Professional Publishing Ltd

ℛ A member of the Reed Elsevier plc group

OXFORD BOSTON JOHANNESBURG
MELBOURNE NEW DELHI SINGAPORE

First published 1997

© Institute of Management Foundation 1997

British Library Cataloguing in Publication Data
A catalogue record for this book is available from the British Library

ISBN 0 7506 3676 9

Typeset by Avocet Typeset, Brill, Aylesbury, Bucks
Printed and bound in Great Britain

Contents

Series overview

The Institute of Management Open Learning Programme is a series of workbooks prepared by the Institute of Management and Pergamon Open Learning for managers seeking to develop themselves.

Comprising seventeen open learning workbooks, the programme covers the best of modern management theory and practice, and each workbook provides a range of frameworks and techniques to improve your effectiveness as a manager, thus helping you acquire the knowledge and skill to make you fully competent in your role.

Each workbook is written by an experienced management writer and covers an important management topic or theme. The activities both reinforce learning and help to relate the generic ideas to your individual work context. While coverage of each topic is fully comprehensive, additional reading suggestions and reference sources are given for those who wish to study to a greater depth.

Designed to be practical, stimulating and challenging, the aim of the workbooks is to improve performance at work by benefiting you and your organization. This practical focus is at the heart of the competence-based approach that has been adopted by the programme.

The structure of the programme

The design and overall structure of the programme has two main organizing principles, both of which are closely linked to the national standards for management developed by the MCI (Management Charter Initiative).

First, the workbooks are grouped according to the key roles of management.

- Underpinning the management standards are a series of **personal competences** which describe the personal skills required by all managers, which are essential to developing skill in all the main functional or key role areas.
- **Manage Activities** describes the principles of managing processes and activities, with service to the customer as an essential part of this.
- **Manage Resources** describes the acquisition, control and monitoring of financial and other resources.
- **Manage People** looks at the key skills involved in leadership, developing one's staff and managing their performance.

■ **Manage Information** discusses the acquisition, storage and use of information for communication, problem solving and decision making.

In addition, there are three specialized key roles: **Manage Quality, Manage Projects** and **Manage Energy**. The workbooks cover the first two of these. Unlike the four primary key roles above, these are not compulsory for certificate, diploma or S/NVQ requirements, but provide options for the latter.

Together, these key roles provide a comprehensive description of the fundamental principles of management as it applies in any organization – commercial, maintained sector or not-for-profit.

Second, the programme is organized according to **levels of management**, seniority and responsibility.

Level 4 represents first line management. In accredited programmes this is equivalent to S/NVQ Level 4, Certificate in Management or CMS. Level 5 is equivalent to middle/senior management and is accredited at S/NVQ Level 5, Diploma in Management or DMS. There are two S/NVQs at Level 5: Operational Management and Strategic Management. The operations role is focused internally within an organization on the maintenance of systems and standards of output, whilst the strategic role is focused on the whole organization, including the external operating environment, and looks at setting directions.

Together, the workbooks cover all the background knowledge you need to have for all units of competence in the MCI standards at Level 4 and Level 5 (apart from the specialized units in the key role Manage Energy). They also provide skills development and opportunities for portfolio building.

For a comprehensive list of workbooks, see pages ix and x. For a comprehensive list of links with the standards, see pages 3 and 40–1.

How to use the programme

The programme is deliberately designed to be flexible and can be used in a variety of ways:

■ to update on important management topics and themes, or develop individual skills: as the workbooks are grouped according to themes, it should be easy for you to pick out one that suits your needs

■ as part of generic management development programmes: you can choose the modules that fit the themes of the programme

■   **as part of, and in support of, accredited competence-based programmes.**

For N/SVQs at both Levels 4 and 5, there are options in the combinations of units that make up the various awards. By using the map provided in the *User Guide*, individuals will be able to select the workbooks appropriate to their specific needs, and their chosen accreditation options. Some of the activities will help you provide evidence for your portfolio; where we think this is the case, we give the relevant reference to the standards.

For Certificate or CMS, Diploma or DMS, individuals should choose modules that not only meet their individual needs but also satisfy the requirements of the delivering body and the awarding body.

You may need help and guidance in these choices, and the *User Guide* sets out the options and advice in much more detail. A fuller description of the potential uses of this material in evidence gathering and portfolio building can also be found in Sections 6 and 7, and a detailed description of the contents of each workbook can be found in Section 2.

Workbooks in the Institute of Management Open Learning Programme

Personal Competences (Levels 4 and 5)

1 *The influential Manager**
2 *Managing Yourself**

Managing Activities (Level 4)

3 *Understanding Business Process Management*
4 *Customer Focus*

Managing Activities (Level 5)

5 *Getting TQM to Work*
6 *Leading from the Front*
7 *Improving your Organization's Success*

Managing Resources (Level 4)

8 *Project Management*
9 *Budgeting and Financial Control*

Managing Resources (Level 5)

10 *Effective Financial and Resource Management*

Managing People (Level 4)

1 *The Influential manager*
2 *Managing Yourself*
11 *Getting the Right People to do the Right Job*

An asterisk indicates that a particular workbook also contains material suitable for a particular key role or personal competence.

The workbooks as linked to the IM modules

Workbook title	IM module	Module guided hours	Module unguided study hours	Certificate/Diploma
The Influential Manager	D4	25	40	Diploma
	M4	20	30	Certificate
Managing Yourself	D4	25	40	Diploma
	M4	20	30	Certificate
Understanding Business Process Management	M2	30	40	Certificate
Customer Focus	D1	40	60	Diploma
	M1	20	30	Certificate
Getting TQM to Work	D1	40	60	Diploma
	D2	30	45	Diploma
Leading from the Front	DE2	20	30	Diploma in Strategic Management
	DE1	20	30	Diploma in Strategic Management
Improving Your Organization's Success	DE3	20	30	Diploma in Strategic Management
Project Management	M3	40	60	Certificate
Budgeting and Financial Control	M3	40	60	Certificate
Effective Financial and Resource Management	D3	25	40	Diploma
Getting the Right People to do the Right Job	D5	30	45	Diploma
	M5	20	30	Certificate
	M7	20	30	Certificate
	M8	30	45	Certificate
Developing Yourself and Your Staff	M6	40	60	Certificate
Building a High Performance Team	D7	40	60	Diploma
	M6	40	60	Certificate
The New Model Leader	DE4	20	30	Diploma in Strategic Management
	D6	30	40	Diploma
	D7	40	60	Diploma
Making Rational Decisions	M8	30	45	Certificate
Communication	M8	30	45	Certificate
Successful Information Management	D8	40	60	Diploma

Certificate/Diploma courses

These open learning workbooks are designed to offer learning centres maximum flexibility, by fitting around different modes of delivery. They can therefore be used as a major part of either the unguided (30–60 hours per module) or guided (20–40 hours per module) study elements of the Certificate/Diploma courses.

Section 1
Introduction to the series

Introduction to the workbooks

The focus of the workbooks is on improving performance at work – benefiting you and your organization. This is the essence of the 'competency-based' approach, where success with the programme is measured by practical evidence from the workplace according to nationally agreed management standards.

The materials in this series have been developed by experienced management writers, and the series has been designed to be practical, stimulating and challenging. The series is also designed to appeal to managers whatever their organization or business. The fundamental principles of management – leading and developing people, managing finance and resources, organizing processes and activities, managing and using information, meeting customer needs, developing personal skills and managing in an efficient, ethical manner – remain the same worldwide, whether in public sector or private, manufacturing or service industry.

The titles at each level provide a full description of the concepts, models, processes and procedures that represent up-to-date management concepts and best practice. There are activities throughout the text that not only reinforce the learning, but also help to provide the basis of evidence for assessment in a competence-based management programme.

Each workbook carries lists of additional reading and reference sources for those who wish to study to a greater depth.

Qualifications

Should you wish to gain formal recognition of your management skills this is also available using successful completion of these materials as a basis. The options are:

■ *Vocational qualifications*
Using practical, work-based activities combined with evidence of your achievements at work to develop a portfolio. This can then be assessed so that you receive a vocational qualification: an internationally recognized qualification confirming your management expertise and competence.

■ *Certificate and Diploma in Management*
The Institute of Management, the largest broadly based management institution in the UK, offers internationally renowned certificates and diplomas in management to candidates who can demonstrate the 'acquisition and practical application of knowledge'. This programme provides the underpinning knowledge needed, whether for a first-line manager at certificate level or a strategic manager at diploma level, and some of the workbook activities and assignments can provide the basis for assessment. These are delivered via a network of college-based providers, or centres which are listed at the back of this book. There is also a range of alternative suppliers and centres who deliver equivalent management qualifications. Most renowned is, from Edexcel, the professional Development Certificate and Diploma; many universities, however, issue their own certificates and diplomas in management. This programme should provide the underpinning knowledge for all management qualifications for first-line, middle or senior managers in the workplace.

Neither qualification route requires an examination, and both qualifications can be obtained if the standards are met. For further details of how to attain these management qualifications see Section 6: Gaining qualifications, and Section 7: The accreditation process.

Who will find it useful?

The Institute of Management Open Learning Programme concentrates on the practical application of management theory and principles in the contexts of the developing, or first-line, manager, and the senior manager or strategist. Certain workbooks cover management skills of particular relevance to the first-line or middle manager, while others focus on techniques for senior managers to employ in developing themselves and their organization. Both approaches provide momentum for continuing personal and professional development.

The authors of the series recognize that a manager rarely operates at only one level and that management careers involve a broad range of tasks and responsibilities. Furthermore, what is important is an understanding of the topic, for example leadership or meeting customer needs; workbook titles therefore relate to management concepts in a lively and interesting style, rather than just the *level* of the manager.

The titles in the series are listed in Table 1, according to their key roles and levels:

Table 1 Workbooks in the Institute of Management Open Learning Programme

	Level 4	Level 5
Manage Activities	3 *Understanding Business Process Management* 4 *Customer Focus*	5 *Getting TQM to Work* 6 *Leading from the Front* 7 *Improving your Organization's Success*
Manage Resources	8 *Project Management* 9 *Budgeting and Financial Control*	10 *Effective Financial and Resource Management*
Manage People	1 *The Influential Manager** 2 *Managing Yourself** 11 *Getting the Right People to do the Right Job* 12 *Developing Yourself and Your Staff* 13 *Building a High Performance Team*	14 *The New Model Leader*
Manage Information	15 *Making Rational Decisions* 16 *Communication*	17 *Successful Information Management*
Personal Competences	1 *The Influential Manager** 2 *Managing Yourself**	
Manage Quality	3 *Understanding Business Process Management** 4 *Customer Focus**	5 *Getting TQM to Work**
Manage Projects	8 *Project Management**	8 *Project Management**

*An asterisk indicates that a particular workbook also contains material suitable for a key role or personal competence.

FIRST-LINE AND MIDDLE MANAGERS

The programme develops the skills of first-line and middle managers: those managers who are at the front line in most modern organizations. They can make the difference between success or failure, action or inaction, as they provide an informed view, shaped by their closeness to the customer and understanding of the work in hand. Their knowledge of processes, customers, colleagues and the efficiency of the business is vital in shaping its organization. This resource can be developed to innovate and strengthen the organization, and this is increasingly the case with the growing number of organizations where management structures are becoming flatter, with fewer hierarchies. Increasingly first-line managers are being asked to undertake more and more tasks and responsibilities, and in the worst cases this is matched by a lack of understanding, motivation or development.

SENIOR MANAGERS AND STRATEGISTS

The programme advances the development of the senior manager by focusing on the strategic issues of managing an organization. In many cases skilful, expert managers are taken from their areas of functional expertise and expected to manage much larger, diverse activities, while even experienced managers face difficult, even turbulent times for which they are largely unprepared. By building upon past knowledge and experience the programme provides the strategic manager with a new, refreshed perspective from which to develop the organization. The workbooks are written with a total quality management approach as the guiding principle, in the belief that this not only effects great change within an organization but leads to a culture of lasting and self-sustaining improvement and development.

Benefits – what the Institute of Management Open Learning Programme can achieve for you

FIRST-LINE AND MIDDLE MANAGERS

This series develops the skills and releases the potential of first-line and middle managers. It will:

- improve personal effectiveness
- lay the foundation for continuing personal and professional development
- support the organization in achieving its objectives
- support a range of internationally recognized management qualifications

SENIOR MANAGERS AND STRATEGISTS

This series supports the aims and aspirations of senior managers. It will help you:

- plan the future development of your organization
- instil a total quality culture
- develop your managers
- lead and initiate change in a profitable way
- support a range of internationally recognized management qualifications

Section 2
Organization of the series

The main feature of the Institute of Management Open Learning Programme is its clear, lively and innovative writing style, perfected by expert authors, editors and a rigorous development process. Developed and endorsed by the Institute of Management, the text is authoritative, covering the knowledge and understanding required, but also explaining modern management concepts and best practice.

The series is divided into four main areas which reflect key management roles. The four areas are:

MANAGE ACTIVITIES

This covers a wide range of skills which are necessary to build a total quality culture. The importance of key concepts is clearly explained and illustrated, including the nature of customer/supplier relationships and customer service; how business processes work and how to improve them; and how to plan, lead and evaluate new initiatives and strategies. Manage Activities is chiefly about ensuring that business operations and activities are efficient and constantly improving, and that customers' needs are being met. The five titles recognize that managers need to be able to:

- manage activities to meet customer requirements
- contribute to the improvement of activities and plans
- implement quality assurance systems
- implement change and improvements in organizational activities
- review internal and external operating environments
- establish strategies to guide the work of the organization
- evaluate and improve organizational performance

MANAGE RESOURCES

This module covers the skills needed to balance the competing demands for different resources – chiefly finance, time and equipment. Techniques are explained for planning, securing, allocating and using resources, and ensuring that the resource plan meets the needs of the organization and customers. The need to budget and control costs, and to understand and use financial techniques to their full advantage, is vital to the success of any organization.

MANAGE PEOPLE

Managing people is often seen as the most important responsibility of management, and without doubt the ability to understand, communicate, motivate and get the best from people is fundamental to succeeding as a manager. It is a complex topic, with as many approaches to managing people as there are people to be managed, but there are universal points to bear in mind and key skills which apply to all managers. The workbook activities will help you to find your own personal management style and how to improve your skills in this area.

MANAGE INFORMATION

Information is the key to survival and competitive advantage, but coping with a bewildering amount of information on a daily basis can be difficult when decisions need to be made quickly and effectively. The three workbooks in this module explain:

- how to achieve control with practical advice and guidelines
- how to manage and send information for effective decision making
- methods for using information to plan and evaluate business success and achieve business improvements

In addition, the following areas designated by the advisory group responsible for the management standards have also been covered:

PERSONAL COMPETENCIES

The workbooks relevant to this area provide essential skills for personal development and effectiveness. The two titles reflect the personal competence model of the national management standards, but more importantly they provide a personal framework for developing management skills. Subjects covered include managing in context and the role of a manager; and the importance of ethical management. Techniques covered include effective decision making, influencing others, managing time and stress, planning your career development and managing yourself.

MANAGE QUALITY

Continuous improvement and quality are critical to business success and are key requirements of managers. The workbooks relevant to this module look at how to ensure you meet the mark as far as quality is concerned.

MANAGE PROJECTS

The workbook relevant to this module covers planning, controlling and concluding projects.

Synopsis of workbooks by management area

MANAGE ACTIVITIES

Manage Activities is divided into five workbooks: two primarily for the first-line and operational managers and three titles which address more senior or strategic issues. The five titles in the Manage Activities area are:

Workbook 3: Understanding Business Process Management
Workbook 4: Customer Focus
Workbook 5: Getting TQM to Work
Workbook 6: Leading from the Front
Workbook 7: Improving Your Organization's Success

Workbook 3: Understanding Business Process Management

Objectives – by the end of this workbook you should be able to:
- explain the importance of business processes and their relationship with quality assurance
- establish systems to monitor quality
- apply techniques to improve business processes

Content – this workbook covers:
- business processes: fishbone diagrams and what processes mean for cost, quality and delivery
- how effective management of processes leads to efficient management of resources
- how to set up systems for monitoring and improvement of product/service quality (and types of system)

Workbook 4: Customer Focus

Objectives – by the end of this workbook you should be able to:
- know your customers: who they are and what they need
- explain the relationship between price, cost and value
- manage your customers so that they return to you
- plan operational activities to meet customer requirements

Content – this workbook covers:
- knowing your customers: who are internal and external customers and suppliers, and how to ascertain their requirements
- the importance of market research and techniques (formal and informal) for effective research
- handling customer contact and the importance of dialogue
- how to plan activities to meet requirements for price, quality and delivery
- customer satisfaction and quality: knowing the hype from best practice and understanding what is required to assure quality, including the importance of soft skills (e.g. attitude and motivation) as well as the harder skills for managing operations

Workbook 5: Getting TQM to Work

Objectives – by the end of this workbook you should be able to:
- explain the four key stages in implementing a successful TQM programme apply the right process management tools
- create the right culture for successful change management programmes
- manage staff to ensure implementation of TQM, effectively communicating, empowering and motivating
- set goals for an effective TQM programme and set up mechanisms for problem solving

Content – this workbook covers:
- understanding, preparing and planning for TQM
- the four stages for implementing TQM
- goal-setting and measuring performance
- problem-solving techniques
- creating the right culture: how to prepare people, communicate goals and achieve ownership
- the role and importance of motivating and empowering people
- techniques for process management including: Pareto analysis, fishbone charts, flowcharts

Workbook 6: Leading from the Front

Objectives – by the end of this workbook you should be able to:
- explain the key elements of organizational culture and how to influence change
- develop and communicate a vision and sense of purpose to all stakeholders
- describe the role of the senior manager, and apply techniques for:
  - organizational planning
  - team building
  - decision making
  - managing knowledge
- benchmark the organization within its operating environment
- develop and implement a strategic plan

Content – this workbook covers:
- understanding the role of the senior manager
- what organizational culture is, benefits and problems, and how to influence the culture of the organization
- how to benchmark an organization
- how to prepare a strategic plan, and the steps needed for effective implementation
- assessing leadership styles and techniques for building a winning team

Workbook 7: Improving Your Organization's Success

Objectives – by the end of this workbook you should be able to:
- apply techniques to measure the organization's strengths and weaknesses, successes and failures
- identify areas for improvement within the organization
- set business policies and approaches to all aspects of management within the organization
- implement techniques to improve organizational effectiveness

Content – this workbook covers:
- undertaking a SWOT analysis
- devising a business plan and action plan for improving performance
- understanding the value of managing change, and adopting measures for continuous improvement
- understanding influences on corporate culture
- ethical approaches to management, including business ethics and the advantages and importance of responsible management

MANAGE RESOURCES

Manage Resources is divided into three titles which look at techniques for planning, allocating and managing resources to meet organizational objectives. The three titles are:

Workbook 8: Project Management
Workbook 9: Budgeting and Financial Control
Workbook 10: Effective Financial and Resource Management

Workbook 8: Project Management

Objectives – by the end of this workbook you should be able to:

- describe the organizational context of resource planning, and how internal and external factors influence the use of resources
- organize team roles and responsibilities
- plan for the effective use of resources
- apply techniques to secure and use resources, including project management and negotiating techniques

Content – this workbook covers:

- organizational factors affecting resources: mission statements; ethics; strategic and business plans; revenue and expenditure budgets
- assigning team roles: introductions to motivating and empowering
- techniques for managing resources: project planning and management tools; monitoring and evaluation skills; negotiating skills

Workbook 9: Budgeting and Financial Control

Objectives – by the end of this workbook you should be able to:

- describe the importance of business planning at different levels (strategic, division and operating plans) and how controlling resources leads to achieving objectives
- apply techniques for financial planning and forecasting, and devise budgets and operational plans
- implement techniques for financial analysis, monitoring and control
- construct and communicate a business case

Content – this workbook covers:

- budgeting: drawing up a budget, controlling a budget
- understanding approaches to strategic and business planning
- financial control and analysis techniques
- forecasting techniques for financial management
- preparing a business case: how to prepare a case to secure resources

Workbook 10: Effective Financial and Resource Management

Objectives – by the end of this workbook you should be able to:

- relate the organization's mission to the allocation of financial resources
- apply techniques for financial management, including financial statements and external sources of finance and capital
- analyse financial information and historical data to monitor performance
- establish and communicate budgets and financial information
- prepare and evaluate business cases for financial resources
- ensure that systems, people and resources are in place to meet objectives

Content – this workbook covers:

- strategic planning techniques
- gaining support and commitment, and communicating organizational plans
- understanding ratios for financial management
- analysing financial data and business plans
- problem-solving techniques and approaches to improving financial performance
- understanding financial statements and accounts, and sources of funds

MANAGE PEOPLE

Manage People is divided into six titles which look at personal skills, team development, and other people management issues. The six titles are:

Workbook 1: The Influential Manager
Workbook 2: Managing Yourself
Workbook 11: Getting the Right People to do the Right Job
Workbook 12: Developing Yourself and Your Staff
Workbook 13: Building a High Performance Team
Workbook 14: The New Model Leader

Workbook 1: The Influential Manager

Objectives – by the end of this workbook you should be able to:

- describe and adopt an ethical approach to management issues which is both open and reasoned
- plan and prioritize objectives
- apply techniques to influence and communicate with colleagues
- apply techniques for decision making

Content – this workbook covers:

- the scope, advantages and disadvantages of codes of ethics, and the steps necessary to adopt an ethical approach

- objective setting: why it is important and how to do it
- ways in which people communicate, including modern technology
- basic communication skills: when to speak, write and listen. Dos and don'ts for effective communication
- steps in the decision-making process

Workbook 2: Managing Yourself

Objectives – by the end of this workbook you should be able to:
- apply the skills required to make decisions and initiate action
- apply techniques to ensure a positive, assertive approach
- describe the nature of stress and apply techniques for stress management
- effectively manage your time
- plan your personal and professional development
- understand your style of learning

Content – this workbook covers:
- techniques for improving assertiveness and dealing with difficult situations and colleagues
- activities to assess and improve decision-making skills
- the causes and effects of stress, and how to channel pressure for positive benefits
- time management techniques
- methods for personal and professional development
- activities to assess learning styles

Workbook 11: Getting the Right People to do the Right Job

Objectives – by the end of this workbook you should be able to:
- apply techniques for recruitment and selection of staff
- state the legal requirements of personnel management, including recruitment, dismissal, and health and safety of staff
- implement a grievance and disciplinary procedure and dismiss staff
- explain the importance of team and organizational culture for effective performance

Content – this workbook covers:
- skills for interviewing, recruitment and selection of staff
- legal aspects of personnel management
- how to work through grievance and disciplinary procedures, and how to dismiss staff
- criteria for choosing and deploying staff for specific functions and projects
- organizational culture: what it is, what it can achieve, how it can be nurtured and how it is damaged

Workbook 12: Developing Yourself and Your Staff

Objectives – by the end of this workbook you should be able to:
- utilize information about the different types of learning style
- describe the Investors in People standard, and
- apply the four principles of development: evaluate and identify training needs; take action; monitor and assess the results; feed back results
- apply skills for mentoring and coaching colleagues

Content – this workbook covers:
- putting staff development in the context of motivation and empowerment
- appreciation and understanding of different learning styles: exercise to identify the individual's learning style
- Kolb's learning cycle
- ways in which people can take responsibility for their own development (it's not just a training course!)
- techniques for effective mentoring
- techniques for effective coaching (one to one)
- techniques for planning and running training sessions (one to several)

Workbook 13: Building a High Performance Team

Objectives – by the end of this workbook you should be able to:
- set direction for your team and maintain control
- describe the value of empowerment, and apply techniques to empower your team
- set objectives and develop your team and your operation to achieve them
- motivate and support staff to achieve objectives

Content – this workbook covers:
- empowerment: what it is and how to properly empower people
- techniques for objective setting
- motivating people: useful tools, best practice and pitfalls
- assessing personal empowerment: how much are you empowered?
- techniques and tools for assessing performance
- how to provide feedback to staff in all circumstances

Workbook 14: The New Model Leader

Objectives – by the end of this workbook you should be able to:
- lead your staff and build teams
- describe your own leadership style
- plan and communicate the aims and objectives for your organization

- delegate and empower staff
- resolve conflict
- assess people's strengths and weaknesses and facilitate development
- solve problems
- plan, support and protect team projects

Content – this workbook covers:
- assessing leadership styles
- setting the mission for the organization, using consensus, and gaining commitment
- tools for assessing staff performance and providing feedback
- approaches to problem solving
- project planning skills and the need to allocate resources
- how to manage and empower high performers
- understanding the range of stakeholders in an organization, and how best to approach them

MANAGE INFORMATION

The three titles in this area cover the topics of communication, solving problems and making decisions. They are:

Workbook 15: Making Rational Decisions
Workbook 16: Communication
Workbook 17: Successful Information Management

Workbook 15: Making Rational Decisions

Objectives – by the end of this workbook you should be able to:
- establish systems and relationships to provide information
- determine information requirements, and develop questioning skills to find out information
- establish systems to manage, store and retrieve information
- make decisions based on information analysis
- communicate information and decisions

Content – this workbook covers:
- gathering information: how to search and evaluate information
- storing data: what to store and how to store
- how and when to deliver information orally, in writing, electronically
- decision-making techniques
- the benefits and pitfalls of information technology

Workbook 16: Communication

Objectives – by the end of this workbook you should be able to:

- deliver information in writing, orally and via electronic media
- communicate effectively through appropriate media
- contribute to meetings and group discussions
- influence and manage colleagues through discussion and persuasion

Content – this workbook covers:

- business and report writing skills, including business proposals
- presentation skills: how to plan and deliver presentations to small and large groups
- chairing meetings
- using technology to communicate, including e-mail, video-conferencing
- communicating using the telephone

Workbook 17: Successful Information Management

Objectives – by the end of this workbook you should be able to:

- explain the importance of managing knowledge and apply appropriate management techniques
- establish requirements for information processes and resources
- evaluate and select systems for information dissemination and management
- assess proposals for information management and implement their introduction
- monitor and evaluate the effectiveness of communication systems
- suggest and implement improvements in information management tools
- describe the legal context of managing information

Content – this workbook covers:

- how to carry out an information audit and assess information needs
- techniques for managing information:
  - measuring the effectiveness of existing systems
  - suggesting improvements to information and communication systems
- how to present proposals for better information management
- how to assess proposals for information systems and technology, gain consensus and implement their introduction
- legal requirements of information management

Section 3 Learning to learn – getting the best from the series

Participating in the Institute of Management Open Learning Programme provides you with an extremely flexible means of study. You incur none of the risks of taking time out from work and your career path is uninterrupted. The programme also offers complete geographical flexibility. In the event of job or location changes you will be certain that you can continue your studies. The programme is specially designed to be followed by managers working anywhere in the world.

With the programme you begin to use your skills and knowledge almost immediately, demonstrating the immensely practical nature of the business expertise contained in the programme. In conjunction with the programme you may wish to pursue the Institute of Management Certificate in Management (for first-line managers); the Diploma in Management (for senior managers); certificates or diplomas from alternative awarding bodies or providers; or a vocational qualification at Level 4 or 5.

Learning to learn

It is extraordinary how little attention we pay to learning; indeed, the only people who are likely to discuss how we learn are people who are learning to teach! The Institute of Management Open Learning Programme is based on a coherent approach to learning: this is reflected in the organization of the workbooks and their approach to each topic. Much school and higher education learning is based on reading books and being told what to do. We feel that management development is not really like that, and that learning is best described as a cycle of activities as shown in Figure 1.

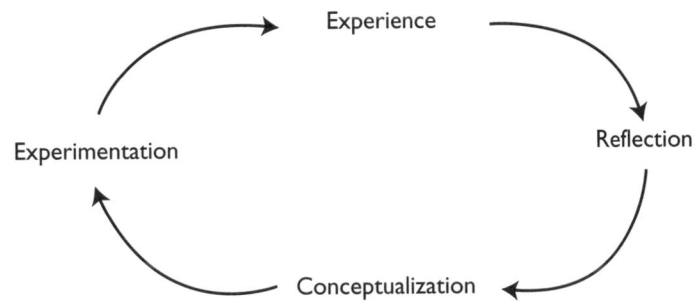

Figure 1   Learning as a cycle of activities

- *Experience* – this of course might be planned or accidental.
- *Reflection* – where we think about our experience and take note of what happens.
- *Conceptualization* – here we generalize and construct theories. We develop ideas on why things happen the way they do.
- *Experimentation* – this is where we test our ideas in new situations.

It might help if you think about some learning from your own experience. How did you learn to make friends and encourage people? Certainly not from a textbook. It is also likely that you learnt most of what you know about management through experience.

The programme helps us to move around the cycle in the following ways:

- by giving **inputs**, including work-based activities, case studies and information from the self-study workbooks
- by providing opportunities to **reflect** on your own experience in the context of new approaches and techniques
- by providing opportunities to **discover** new ideas, skills or ways of achieving things

By using your own experience and by providing the right learning opportunities we can make the programme a worthwhile and relevant experience.

Managing your own learning

As part of the programme you will be developing your own personal effectiveness skills. One important aspect of personal effectiveness is the management of your own learning and development. Obviously you will get better at it as you go along and with experience, but here are several key points to bear in mind:

- *Set achievable goals* – it is important to set goals which are SMART: specific, measurable, action-oriented, realistic, and time constrained. You need to decide what you wish to achieve and use the programme to help you.
- *Study regularly* – research shows that people's efficiency in learning and remembering from written materials is less if study periods are too long. A little and often is a good rule of thumb.
- *Plan your sessions* – plan on doing an identifiable amount of work (such as a section) and give yourself a timetable.
  Manage your time – set aside the time for studying and try to ensure that there aren't other calls on your time.
- *Review* – regularly review your progress: not only how much you have studied but how well you have been able to apply it in practice.
- *Organization* – make sure that you can put your hands on any pens, paper, notes, reference materials, etc. that you may need.
- *Environment* – make sure that you are comfortable and that the light is good; ensure that you environment is free from distractions. Take frequent breaks.
- *Support* – get the support of family, friends and colleagues so that they know and understand what you are doing.
- *Active involvement* – you will make more of your learning if you complete the activities as you go along, and make notes to summarize main points to refer to later.

Perhaps most importantly, make sure that you *understand* what you learn, and think of how best to *apply* it. Take time to think and reflect – don't just rush through the work but try and think of the most important applications of each concept.

Effective learning requires both understanding and use:

- to truly learn anything you have to *understand* it
- to remember, you have to *use* it

You will therefore gain most from your studying if you apply the techniques that you have learnt to your work situation, and this is best done with the support of colleagues and those working with you.

Gaining support from others

To get the best out of the programme you will almost certainly need the support of others around you for a wide variety of reasons both personal and practical. The cast of characters who should be involved includes:

MENTOR

The principal role of a mentor could be described as promoting the circumstances for you to gain the confidence, skills, attitudes and opportunities to manage and develop your own learning. This requires the mentor to fulfil the roles at various times of counsellor, confidante, facilitator or creative problem solver, advisor and communication channel.

Of course, you can study the programme without a mentor, but in practice most people find learning easier with such support. Many organizations have mentoring schemes in place for their staff, whether managerial or not, because of the benefits that such a scheme provides. It need not be a bureaucratic or even a formal arrangement: successful mentoring means providing a sounding board and a source of guidance, reflection and advice, and this can be achieved just as well through informal discussions as by a structured arrangement.

Your mentor is likely to be a more experienced manager than you and may have specialist functional or technical skills which you can benefit from. However, they will not be a specialist on every possible subject and you shouldn't expect them to be. They are likely to have influence within your organization and should be the route to the help and expertise you need.

The practical support that you might expect from a mentor includes:

- help in setting learning objectives
- an understanding of the requirements of the programme and help in gaining the support of your organization so you can meet the requirements
- help in structuring your learning programme and managing your time
- constructive and assertive feedback
- advice about evidence and assessment (for competency-based qualifications)
- help in solving problems and creating opportunities

FAMILY AND FRIENDS

The support and understanding of family and friends is vitally important: it can provide an objective view of a particular situation, and prevent any misunderstanding about why you are doing the programme and what it involves. Explaining your objectives, the purpose of the programme and how you will benefit will show the advantages of the Institute of Management Open Learning Programme. Remember, too, that it is important to have a life outside work and to relax and unwind, to ensure that you are fully effective, whether working or studying.

LINE MANAGER

You will get more from the programme and you will find life easier if you can obtain the cooperation and involvement of your line manager. They are a possible source of help and advice, and they may hold the key to some important learning opportunities for you. In order for you to get their involvement you should discuss the programme with them at an early stage, and keep them up to date with your progress and activities.

ASSESSOR

If you are studying for a competency-based qualification you will be told who your assessor is at an early stage. You may even have the opportunity to meet with them and discuss any questions you have. It is also possible, and in many cases advisable to send them 'sighting shots' of work for your assignments or portfolios.

PERSONNEL PROFESSIONAL; PROJECT MANAGER

On many in-company programmes there is usually someone who is responsible for coordination between you, the trainer and assessor. They should be a good source of advice about practical issues. One of their functions will be to organize the timetable of activities.

TUTOR

If you are studying on a structured qualification programme your tutor will provide an important link between the techniques learnt in the self-study materials and your development at work. You should make clear anything you don't understand or need clarifying, and don't be afraid to discuss the *application* of tools and techniques with your tutor.

Whether studying as part of a group or individually it is worth remembering that what you get out of the programme depends very heavily on what you contribute in terms of time, thought and effort. All of the people mentioned above can be an essential source of guidance, advice and information, but they can only support *your* efforts.

Section 4   How to use the series to improve management effectiveness

How to combine individual and organizational development – the programme linked to organizational objectives

Before you start to study the Institute of Management Open Learning Programme, if you are sponsored or supported by your organization, the senior managers within your organization should have agreed the objectives and issues that they want the programme to address. This process sets the framework for the programme within the organization and provides the means to evaluate its success. Once the key issues to be addressed have been decided, the programme is designed to enable managers to learn and apply techniques which will initiate change and achieve results through work-based activity. In this way studying and then applying management skills and techniques from the programme, together with your manager and mentor, will blend your development with that of the organization.

The programme requires you to think about your daily activities, and draws its content from your own work and experiences. If you are studying as part of a group then this will complement the direct and individual relevance of the programme.

The way that the self-study materials are used will probably depend on your organization and tutor, but it is important that you agree with your mentor what the *overall* programme requires and what is expected of you. In addition to the self-study workbooks two types of task might be required:

- *Development tasks* – these are learning tasks (usually in the workplace) designed to develop skills that you do not currently have. For instance, if you have never been involved in recruitment and selection, you may need to go through the process of interviewing to develop competence.

■ *Assessment tasks* – it is possible in some circumstances that you will need to create the opportunity to demonstrate a competence that is not currently part of your job specification for the purposes of assessment. You may also need to undertake a work-based project to provide evidence of competence.

It is possible that you will not need either of these for any or all of the work-books. In any event you should not worry if these ideas sound unfamiliar – your mentor is there to help you.

The key features of work-based and self-study learning

The work-based and self-study learning approach adopted by this series offers a number of important advantages over traditional taught programmes and courses of study. These include:

■ The facility to learn:
   a) at your own pace
   b) in an environment that is best suited to your needs
   c) in your own time and work time
■ Learning throughout the year, on a continuous basis, allows the information to be both absorbed and applied more readily. Skills and knowledge are thereby increased in parallel.
■ The opportunity to discover latent talents that were not apparent before. This stems from being able to continue development in a practical, work-based environment beyond further education.
■ The skills and knowledge that are learnt and applied are directly relevant to you and your job. They improve your effectiveness and success by focusing on *your* needs: not those of the class or syllabus.

It is also worth noting some of the benefits of work-based and self-study learning for the organization (which mirror those advantages for the individual):

■ training and development can be provided all year round, on demand
■ financial savings are made on travel and accommodation costs
■ learning undertaken is integrated in to the job faster and better when it occurs at the workplace or on a continuous basis, rather than when it is 'time away on a course'

- people become more flexible in their skills and attitudes from continuous learning
- individuals can be released to learn while still fitting in with their workloads and not being absent from work for any length of time
- more responsibility is engendered in managers and their staff for their own training and development when they control the learning process.

Section 5 Which workbooks to study and why – selecting a development programme

Checklist for Personal Development Planning

Before you embark on this programme we suggest that you prepare your *Personal Development Plan* (PDP). This results from identifying the need for skills, knowledge or competence, and defines the appropriate development to meet those perceived needs. A PDP facilitates motivation, monitoring and evaluation of achievements, and provides a schedule to work to.

1. *Find out where you are*

   The starting point should be a self-assessment exercise in terms of skills, employment, qualifications, responsibilities and achievements. This will provide a useful base-line to measure improvements. It is important when measuring your performance to assess *what you can do* as a result of your development activities, and not simply how much time is spent on it. It may help to discuss your strengths and weaknesses with others, for instance family, friends, and your manager.

ACTIVITY 1

Take some time now to reflect on your strengths and your development needs, and write them here.

---

2. *Identify your goals*

Ask what you want to be able to achieve and where you want to be in the future: both short and long term. Map out the steps that will enable you to realize your goals. Be realistic rather than idealistic.

What is the probability of each of these steps coming about? What can you do to influence them?

If it is difficult to identify a particular goal for the future, think about:

- your personal preferences involving private life and family, work and money, constraints and obstacles to mobility and success, now and in the future
- the characteristics of work, such as preferences for managing and working with others versus working alone; working where you are currently or moving to another department or job

ACTIVITY 2

List here your own most important goals. You might want to make distinction between:

- goals in general for yourself
- goals in relation to career

3. *Compare your current profile against these goals and identify development needs*

It is essential as a manager that you take responsibility for identifying and assessing your own development needs. These needs vary over time and may arise from:

- a new or changed job role
- new technology or management
- formal performance appraisal systems
- external assessment – for instance as part of a training needs analysis, skills audit or assessment of prior learning (APL)
- review of performance failures
- periodic review annually, or following events such as promotion, job applications or job loss

Remember, your development needs will differ depending on your career goals.

You may wish to achieve promotion; tackle a new area of work or business opportunity; or simply improve your competence in a specific area of work such as leading people, managing stress, negotiating or communicating.

ACTIVITY 3

Make a statement of those development needs.

4. *Reconsider development needs and convert them into learning objectives*
    For each of the gaps you have identified, set yourself development objectives. These need to be SMART: Specific, Measurable, Achievable, Realistic, Timely. There must be an element of challenge in them so that they stretch you as an individual and take you forward; but they must also be attainable and viable within a realistic time frame, otherwise time will overtake you.

ACTIVITY 4

In the table below list your development needs identified in Activity 3, complete the table by listing your development objectives.

Development need	Development objective

You may wish to develop a learning contract with your manager or mentor, which sets out what you intend to achieve from the programme. Your learning contract might include the following headings:

- purpose of the task
- description of the task

- completion date (if possible)
- outcomes (to be completed after the activity)
- description of the likely evidence
- units/elements claimed (if seeking a vocational qualification)

ACTIVITY 5

Complete the sample learning contract outlined below:

Purpose of task

Description of task

Completion date

Description of likely evidence

Units/elements claimed

---

5. *Identify the possible options*

   List the skills and knowledge you will need to acquire to achieve each of the development needs that you have listed. Compare this list to your current skills and knowledge base and identify the gaps. You will need to consider:

   - *your learning style* – for example some of us learn best from having a go at new experiences, while others prefer to sit back and observe
   - *resources available* – think laterally when trying to identify sources of help for development: during this programme you may find that colleagues, customers and suppliers are all willing to help you with activities which benefit both you and the organization.

ACTIVITY 6

Complete the following table

Development needs	Skills and knowledge required	Sources of new skills and knowledge

---

6. *Monitor your progress*

   Record not only your planned intentions but also your development experiences and their outcomes, both positive and negative. Your personal evaluation of and reflections on learning experiences are essential to this, and more important than merely recording hours spent. Keep copies of evidence which will demonstrate your competence to a potential assessor or manager.

7. *Revise and update the plan*

   Review your plan throughout your career, and at least once a year. Reassess your goals honestly, taking account of any changes in your own priorities, and ensure they are still valid. Revisit your objectives and update them to take account of organizational and technological changes.

Selecting your own development programme

Having assessed your own needs and priorities you should now match these against the workbooks in the series. The series is divided into five broad areas or topics, and the workbooks in each area *either* focus on subjects which are chiefly of interest to first-line or middle managers (which is labelled Level 4), *or* topics likely to meet the needs of senior or strategic managers (which is labelled Level 5).

It is important that you decide first which subjects are those where you need to improve your skills and achieve a greater knowledge and understanding. It may be the case that your needs go across all subjects, in which case simply select the appropriate level and workbooks.

Alternatively, you may wish to improve your techniques in one specific core skill, for instance managing resources, in which case you simply select the appropriate level or workbooks in that area.

Remember, it is important to discuss and agree with your manager, mentor and those running the programme what it aims to achieve, both for you and your organization.

Key features of the materials

The workbooks offer a number of key features:

1. a practical tool to enable you to develop and apply professional skills in the workplace through specific activities
2. the underpinning knowledge which you actually need to develop new skills and to function effectively as a professional manager
3. an account of best practice and discussion on issues that currently influence and affect managers
4. each workbook stands alone with minimum overlap with others in the series, to ensure maximum flexibility of use

The overall aim is to support you in learning and applying skills in the context of your current job in order to become increasingly competent and successful.

Each workbook includes the following:

- *Contents list; series overview; links to the standards*
- *Introduction* – what is the subject about; what does it mean in practice, and why is it important?
- *Objectives* – what you should be able to do by the end of the workbook
- *Sections* – the main text is divided into sections, each containing:
  a) introduction
  b) explanation and information about the topic
  c) activities – either regular activities, which test knowledge and understanding and reinforce learning points, or evidence-generating activities which perform much the same function but also provide additional material from the workplace which you may wish to include in a portfolio of evidence for assessment
  d) case studies
  e) A summary – a short checklist of the aims of that section and key learning points
- *Summary* – an overview of the key learning points
- *Recommended reading* – a detailed reading list should you wish to study the subject further
- *Information about the Institute of Management*

Key uses of the material

There are a number of ways in which the Institute of Management Open Learning Programme can be used:

- as part of a structured management development programme, leading to a vocational qualification (VQ) at Level 4 or 5, or a Certificate or Diploma in Management or CMS or DMS
- to support self-development as part of an individual's continuing personal and professional development
- as part of a structured management development programme, leading to organizational improvements but without providing management qualifications

In the next section we shall explore ways of using the material for a qualification-based programme. However, if you are not (at least at this stage) intent on gaining a qualification, if you follow the advice given in this section and plan your development, you should be able to find workbooks that are particularly suited to your needs. You need to focus on the particular area or areas of expertise you wish to acquire, such as project management, budgeting, influencing skills or TQM, and select a workbook which covers that area. Once you are clear about your development needs, look at the synopsis of each workbook in Section 2 and select accordingly.

Section 6 Using the Institute of Management Open Learning Programme to help gain qualifications

As indicated in the previous section, this programme can be used by those who wish to help gain a qualification in management. This section will show you how.

Study routes and available qualifications

Table 2 indicates the wide range of qualifications at all management levels and will help you decide the most relevant qualification for your level.

Certificates or vocational qualifications?

The Institute of Management Open Learning Programme can support the awards of **both** Certificate/Diploma **and** an NVQ/SVQ. The programme provides complete coverage of the knowledge and understanding requirements of the occupational standards devised by the Management Charter Initiative: the government sponsored lead body for management in the UK.

Table 2 Management qualifications

Candidate's role	Academic/professional qualification	Vocational qualification (National Vocational Qualification (NVQ) Scottish Vocational Qualification (SVQ))
Senior or general manager	Diploma in Management and/or Post Graduate Diploma/Diploma in Management Studies	NVQ/SVQ Level 5 in Management (both Operational and Strategic)
First-line to middle manager	Certificate in Management/Certificate in Management Studies	NVQ/SVQ Level 4 in Management
Owner manager	Certificate in Management (*Owner Management*)/ Certificate in Management Studies	NVQ/SVQ Level 4 in Management (*Business Management and Development*)
Specialist area of management	Certificate in Management (*Managing Quality*) and other specialist and supplementary certificates	NVQ/SVQ additional units
Entrepreneur planning to set up own business	Certificate in Management (*Business Start-up*)/ Certificate in Management Studies	NVQ/SVQ Level 3 (*Business Planning*)

There are key differences between the qualifications:

CERTIFICATES/DIPLOMAS

The IM Certificate and Diploma are described on page 34–6. Because they are devised from the MCI standards they provide an ideal framework for developing and demonstrating management knowledge and skills.

NVQs/SVQs

The occupational standards also include performance criteria which, together with the knowledge specifications, have to be satisfied for the award of an NVQ or SVQ. Assessment is by reference to the candidate's actual performance (or 'competence') in the place of work.

NVQs and SVQs therefore require you to demonstrate *not only* that you 'know how to...' but also that you 'can do...'. Vocational qualifications are awarded only on the basis of naturally occurring, or real, evidence of having met the performance criteria described in the occupational standards.

ELIGIBILITY

In practice, many candidates elect for both the certificate/diploma qualification and the relevant vocational qualification. However, the selection criteria can differ. You should check with providers for the specific requirements.

A key benefit of this programme is that many of the workbook activities are designed to initiate practical improvements in your work, and collecting evidence of these will enable you to achieve a vocational qualification.

The Institute of Management is unique in several respects:

- *Professional status* As soon as you enrol on an Institute of Management programme you will gain free student membership of the Institute for the duration of the programme (up to two years). Membership of the Institute will provide you with access to professional support and opportunities for personal development in company with many of the Institute's 75 000 members – managers from a diverse range of organizations.

- *Support* A unique Personal Portfolio Manager is provided to each candidate who has enrolled on an Institute of Management programme. This 'filofax' contains details of the programme for which you have enrolled, including occupational standards plus reading lists and general guidance on studying and personal development.

The Institute of Management is the largest broadly based management institution in the UK and has offices in London and Corby, but it reaches out to every corner of the globe. It collects, analyses and publishes the collective views of management on matters of topical interest or concern, representing these views to government and other executive bodies.

A list of centres which run management development programmes and provide certificates, diplomas and vocational qualifications is included at the back of this guide. For information about availability and enrolment please contact the Institute of Management programme director at your preferred Institute of Management approved centre.

Other awarding bodies

As well as the Institute of Management there are other organizations who also award certificates, diplomas (including CMS and DMS) and vocational qualifications. The range of possibilities include Edexcel and the RSA which offer awards covering a range of occupational areas including management; to more specialist awarding bodies such as the Institute of Personnel and Development and the Management Verification Consortium.

To offer a vocational programme the provider (usually colleges) need to be approved and registered with an awarding body. It is not the National Council for Vocational Qualifications (NCVQ) that approves the centre: approval comes from the Awarding Bodies to whom authority has been delegated.

The CMS and DMS are awarded by a number of organizations, including Edexcel and many universities. Edexcel's CMS is called Professional Development Certificate in Management Studies, and is aimed particularly at those at an early stage of their management career; it can also be used for underpinning knowledge for an S/NVQ. Edexcel's DMS (Professional Development Diploma in Management Studies) is aimed at middle/senior management and likewise provides underpinning knowledge for an S/NVQ.

The Institute of Management Certificate in Management

The emphasis of this programme is on the **tactical** aspects of management. The programme is aimed at the hands-on manager who has the authority and personal skills to direct operations and to contribute towards the organizational strategy. It is equally valuable for the person who aspires to such a role. In the syllabuses that follow, the role is described as 'the manager' while the members of staff who report to the candidate are described as 'team members' or 'personnel'.

The aim is to enable the operational manager to improve the effectiveness and efficiency of the operations for which they are responsible by means of:

- optimum tactical ulitilization of resources
- effective communication
- development of the team as a coherent, mutually supportive and motivated group of people who, with the manager, share a common vision and purpose as to the nature of their business

Module number	Title
M1	Control of Quality, Safety and Outputs
M2	Continuous Improvement
M3	Planning and Control of Physical and Financial Resources
M4	Development of Personal Management Style
M5	Recruitment and Selection

M6	Planning and Controlling the Work of Teams and Individuals
M7	Managing the Performance of Teams and Individuals
M8	Meetings and Decision Making

The Institute of Management Diploma in Management

The emphasis of this programme is on **operational aspects of strategic** management. The programme is aimed at the middle to senior manager who has the authority and personal inspiration to develop organizational strategy. It is equally valuable for the person who aspires to such a role. In the syllabuses that follow, the role is described as 'the manager' while the members of staff who report to the candidate are described as 'team members' or 'the management team'.

The aim is to enable the strategic manager to impove the competitiveness of the organization for which they are responsible by means of:

- optimum strategic utilization of resources
- effective communication within and outside the organization
- development of the management team as a coherent, mutually supportive and motivated group of people who, with the strategic manager, share a common vision and purpose as to the nature of their business

Module number	Title
D1	Planning and Control
D2	Quality and Safe Systems
D3	Procurement and Effective Use of Resources
D4	Management and Self-development
D5	Recruitment and Redeployment
D6	Organizational Objectives and Teams
D7	Performance Management
D8	Information and Communication Systems

The Institute of Management Diploma in Strategic Management

The emphasis of this programme is on **strategic** management. The programme is aimed at the general manager or director who has the authority and personal skills to implement orgranizational stategy. It is equally valuable for the person who aspires to such a role. In the syllabuses that follow, the role is described as 'the manager' while the members of staff who report to the candidate are described as 'team members' or 'the management team'. The aim is to enable the manager to improve the competitiveness of the organization for which they are responsible by means of:

■ optimum strategic ulitilization of resources
■ effective communication within and outside the organization
■ development of the management team as a coherent, mutually supportive and motivated group of people who, with the strategic manager, share a common vision and purpose as to the nature of the business

Module number	Title
DE1	Review Internal and External Operating Environments
DE2	Operational Strategies
DE3	Evaluate and Improve Organizational Performance
DE4	Delegation and the Development of Managers

Plus Diploma in Management (eight modules)

Open or guided learning

The IM programme, along with those of other awarding and delivering bodies, include these components, which involve amongst other things, the use of open learning workbooks. The appropriate use of these materials should satisfy the requirements of self-study.

NVQs and SVQs at Levels 4 and 5

Vocational qualifications are awarded on the basis of competence demonstrated in the real environment of the workplace. In the context of management the candidate claims competence by reference to specific roles, achievements, projects or other evidence from the work environment, cross-referenced to the occupational standards in a personal portfolio.

NVQs and SVQs are modular so that you may enrol for the full qualification or choose just one or two specific units. Successful assessment in any one unit leads to the award of an NVQ/SVQ Unit Certificate by the Institute of Management. To achieve the vocational qualification at Level 4 or 5, all you have to do is to provide evidence that you can perform the specified activities to the standards shown.

NVQ/SVQ IN MANAGEMENT AT LEVEL 4

The Level 4 vocational qualification in management is intended for the first-line or middle manager who is able to demonstrate competence at this level of seniority in four key areas: Manage Activities; Manage Resources; Manage People and Manage Information. New key role areas are Manage Projects and Manage Quality (both areas are covered by this series) and Manage Energy.

NVQ/SVQ IN MANAGEMENT AT LEVEL 5

There are two vocational qualifications in management at Level 5: S/NVQ Level 5 Management (Operations) and S/NVQ Level 5 (Strategy).

The operations award has a similar structure to the Level 4 award in that candidates take core units, plus optional units across the key roles (including Manage Projects, Manage Quality and Manage Energy).

The strategy award comprises the mandatory units across the key roles: Manage Activities, Manage Resources, Manage People and Manage Information.

The structure of vocational qualifications

Vocational qualifications comprise of statements of competence or 'can do' statements that describe the ability to perform tasks in particular job roles. The awards are based on job roles, are assigned a level, e.g. S/NVQ Level 4 Management.

Each award is broken down into a set of units of competence. This in turn can be divided into a set of individual elements. An element describes what a person should be able to do at work, in language which makes sense to the people who use it. e.g.:

Unit	Element
C2 Develop your own resources	C2.1 Develop yourself to improve performance
	C2.2 Manage your own time and resources to meet your objectives

Each element comes with:

■ *Performance criteria* which describes the outcomes or standards by which competence will be assessed

■ *Range statements* which specify the contexts or circumstances in which the element might be performed

■ *Knowledge and understanding* specifications, which describe the underpinning knowledge required

■ *Evidence requirements* which specify evidence needed for assessment

Assessment

Assessment is an important issue in any qualification structure. One of the distinctive characteristics of the NVQ system is the need for those individuals carrying out assessment activities to be accredited as assessors. The portfolio of evidence which you provide, and which may well be influenced and developed at work as a result of your studies on this programme, will be reviewed by an assessor in order for you to receive your award. Credit can also be given on a unit by unit basis. This is a dealt with in more detail in Section 7: The accreditation process.

ASSESSMENT OF CERTIFICATE AND DIPLOMA

Certificates and Diplomas that are not related to VQs are usually assessed mainly by written assignment (together with a variety of other assessment procedures: including case studies, projects, etc.). A Diploma/DMS may also require a major project or dissertation.

For most certificate or diploma programmes you will need to submit written assignments to be externally assessed. They are used to show that you have grasped the knowledge and understanding of the principles of management within your own work context.

You need to check the specific requirements for the programme or award you are following. The best model for the format of such an assignment is a management report or presentation to your board of directors, stakeholders or your superiors. It will be judged on the quality of the analysis and the structure of the report/presentation. It should include any feedback you receive.

They will normally be assessed against a set of criteria like the following:

■ analysis
■ content and scope
■ report efficiency

There are a number of features that assessors of such assignments like to see:

- good quality information and research in a well-structured and logical order
- good demonstration of knowledge and understanding of the models, frameworks and tools set out in the workbooks
- insightful and relevant accounts of your own experience
- reflection on your own experience and your own learning

Good reports that relate to real working experience tend to:

- *describe* situations, ideas, processes
- *evaluate* or analyse what is happening
- *recommend* or conclude from experience

It is worth remembering and avoiding the most common faults of written assignments:

1. *Excessive length* – stick to the key points and don't dwell on background information or irrelevancies.
2. *Lacking target or focus* – it is easy to get off the point and onto another point, which may be equally important, but don't! Remember the subject of the assignment, its purpose, and present your points clearly and succinctly.
3. *Lack of detail and too many generalities* – you need to present detailed evidence in support of your arguments: lacking detail means you either lose focus or lack credibility and skate over the top of a subject.
4. *Poor structure* – it is certainly well worth planning your assignment before starting, making sure that all the points are covered and lead on from each other in a coherent, rational style. This is also important as you progress through the assignment over a period of time, so that you don't lose your way.

Because you may not have written an assignment report before (or for a very long time) it is possible, by negotiation with the assessor, to send a 'sighting shot' for their comments. Many people find this helpful and reassuring.

Qualifications and assessment summary

- The workbooks can be used for first-line and middle managers – Level 4, and senior managers – Level 5.
- The workbooks satisfy the requirements of vocational qualifications (VQs) and academic qualifications (CMS, DMS). Some programmes (such as those of the Institute of Management) combine VQ Level 4 with Certificate, and VQ Level 5 with Diploma.
- The workbooks satisfy not only the requirements of the Institute of

Management accredited management programmes, but also those of other awarding and delivering bodies.

■ Assessment for VQs is by portfolio of evidence, and this is dealt with in the next section.

■ Assessment for Certificate and Diploma is usually done mainly by written assignment – the guidance for which is in this section.

Table 3 outlines a map which shows how the programme links in with the national standards.

Table 3 The workbooks as linked to units of competence, key roles and levels

Workbook no.	Workbook title	Unit of competence	Key role[1]	Level[2]
1	The Influential Manager	C2, C3	People; Personal Competencies	4, 5
2	Managing Yourself	C5, C6	People; Personal Competencies	4, 5
3	Understanding Business Process Management	A4	Activities; Quality	4
4	Customer Focus	A2, A3	Activities	4
5	Getting TQM to Work	A3, A5, F1–F7	Activities; Quality	5
6	Leading from the Front	A6, A7	Activities	5
7	Improving your Organization's Success	A8	Activities	5
8	Project Management	B2, G1–G6	Resources; Projects	5
9	Budgeting and Financial Control	B3	Resources	5
10	Effective Financial and Resource Management	B4, B5	Resources	5
11	Getting the Right People to do the Right Job	A2, A3, C8, C15, C16, C17	People	4
12	Developing Yourself and Your Staff	C10	People	4
13	Building a High Performance Team	C13	People	4
14	The New Model Leader	C11, C14	People	5
15	Making Rational Decisions	D4	Information	4
16	Communication	D2, D3, D4	Information	4
17	Successful Information Management	D5, D6	Information	5

1 The term key role applies also to the Institute of Management Certificate and Diploma in Management.

2 Levels 4 and 5 refer to the S/NVQ: however, for Level 4 read also Certificate and for Level 5 read also Diploma.

Table 4 shows a complete list of the standards and the qualifications which they comprise, along with the workbooks in which they are covered.

Table 4 Workbooks linked to standards and qualifications

	L4	L4 QM	L5 Operations	L5 Strategy	Dealt with in workbook L4	Dealt with in workbook L5
A2	C	✓			4, 11	
A3			C		4, 11	5
A4	C				3	
A5			C			5
A6				C		6
A7				C		6
A8				C		7
B2	C ✓	✓			8	
B3	C ✓				9	
B4		✓	C			10
B5			✓	C		10
C2	C	C			1	1
C3				C	1	1
C5	C	✓			2	2
C6			C	C	2	2
C8	✓		✓		11	
C10	✓	✓	✓		12	
C11				C		14
C13	✓	✓	✓		13	
C14				C		14
C15	✓		✓		11	
C16			✓		11	
C17			✓		11	
D2	✓	✓	✓		16	
D3			✓	C	16	
D4	C	✓			15	
D5			✓			17
D6			C	C		17
F1		✓	✓			5
F2	✓	C				5
F3		C	✓			5
F4	✓	C	✓			5
F5		C				5
F6	✓	C	✓			5
F7	✓	✓				5
G1	✓		✓		8	
G2	✓		✓		8	
G3	✓		✓		8	
G4			✓			8
G5			✓			8
G6			✓			8

C = Core

✓ = Option

L4 = Level 4

L4 QM = Level 4 Quality Management

L5 Ops = Level 5 Operational Management

L5 Strat = Level 5 Strategic Management

Section 7   The accreditation process

Part One: Developing a portfolio

THE IMPORTANCE OF STARTING EARLY

You may be asking what is a portfolio, and why is it important?

A portfolio is a collection of evidence for the key roles (Manage Activities; Manage People; Manage Resources; Manage Information; Manage Quality; Manage Projects; Manage Energy). It is your portfolio that will be submitted for assessment, and the evidence is the means by which you prove that you have achieved competence to the required standards of performance. The evidence might be direct, which is evidence you produce for yourself, or indirect, which is evidence produced about you by others.

Examples of the **sources of direct evidence** include:

- minutes of meetings
- memos sent
- project reports
- leaflets produced
- letters of satisfaction from customers
- budgets that you have produced
- contracts administered by you
- purchase specifications
- training plans administered by you
- staff appraisals
- job description
- conference papers and publications which you may have contributed to
- business plans
- personal action plans
- health and safety audits

Examples of the **sources of indirect evidence** include statements of verification or testimony provided by:

- line managers
- past and present customers
- training officers
- directors

PORTFOLIO ACTIVITY

Developing a portfolio is an important task which requires careful preparation and planning. It may be worth getting hold of the MCI standards (available from the Management Charter Initiative, see address at the back of this book), identifying one or two of your achievements over the last two years, and reviewing them against the standards. You may find that these achievements cover the requirements.

DISADVANTAGES OF PORTFOLIOS

Before starting you need to ask yourself whether the accreditation process and developing a portfolio is right for you, and whether you will be able to cope. These are questions worth asking yourself as the portfolio process will involve commitment, determination and drive. The disadvantages of preparing a portfolio is that it can be:

- a rather lonely experience, especially if only a few individuals are involved
- retrospective – examining what you have already achieved (you and your manager and mentor need to identify the areas for future development)
- time consuming and rather bureaucratic;
- not easy to achieve without sufficient guidance on how to manage the process

It is important to note that these are general criticisms and should not apply to you if you have determination and experienced professionals to support you.

ADVANTAGES OF PORTFOLIOS

Portfolios:

- can offer experienced managers, without the time and inclination to go back to college, the possibility of gaining formal qualifications
- ensures that managers gain some form of recognition for their normal work (if their portfolios are assessed)
- can add an edge to special initiatives or projects if added to the process of organizational development
- offers a route to other qualifications, such as certificates, diplomas and MBAs
- can switch managers on to the idea of continuing personal and professional development

GETTING STARTED

There is very little prescription about how your evidence is collected, organized and presented. It is therefore a creative communication challenge. Clearly it must have structure and organization. Some people find it easier to plan the structure of their portfolio first and then collect the evidence, while others find it easier to collect evidence and then superimpose a structure.

A good way to make a start on this process is to take an overview of your own job role. In this way you can begin the process of self-assessment and make some early judgments about the strength and scope of your evidence. The Job Role Audit will not only help you to initiate your analysis but will provide a good overview for the assessor. We therefore suggest that you include a completed copy in your portfolio. The Job Role Audit should include the following headings:

Organizational information

Organization:

Name:

Sector:

Size (number of employees):

Nature of business:

Mission:

Organization structure (draw an organizational chart or matrix to show the structure of the organization you work in. Indicate where you fit in to this structure).

Curriculum vitae

Qualifications:

Provide the following information about your employment history, in reverse chronological order (i.e. current job first):

From: _____   To: _____

Job title:

Job description:

Key tasks:

Key achievements:

Key skills:

Number of subordinates:

Deliverables

If you were being appraised today, on what basis would you be judged, and what must you deliver over the course of the next year?

It is important in preparing your portfolio that you plan ahead first; make sure that you have the time and the professional support necessary, and start gathering evidence regularly and as soon as it is available.

CRITERIA OF ACCEPTABLE EVIDENCE

The scope of evidence that is acceptable for assessment is considerable, but there are guidelines and rules for what may and may not be included. Broadly speaking, performance evidence covers two categories: workplace evidence and simulations.

The NCVQ guidelines for NVQ assessment have always emphasized the importance of evidence from the workplace. For example, the 1991 guide states:

performance must be demonstrated and assessed under conditions as close as possible to those under which it would normally be practised – preferably in the workplace.

Unfortunately, in today's rapidly changing work environment it is difficult to establish what the workplace is for many people. Many aspects of creative work are done away from home, particularly for first-line and senior managers. Feedback surveys by companies such as Digital, Rank Xerox and Mercury show that being able to spend a proportion of time at home, with portable kit so as to stay in touch with the office is considered immensely beneficial. Stephen Jupp, Head of Flexible Working at Digital has commented, 'Home is perceived as a quality environment: it is where people feel they are at their most productive.'

The guidelines go on to state that:

… if assessment in the workplace is not practicable, simulations, tests, projects or assignments may provide suitable evidence – but care must be taken to ensure that all elements and performance criteria have been covered, and that it is possible to predict that the competence assessed can be sustained in performance.

In practice case study simulations, tests, observations, interviews, work-based projects and assessment centres are all options for assessment, and are valid in producing evidence. Simulations are often considered to be opportunities to test individuals in activities which are not demonstrable in the workplace. This is often because they deal with contingencies that hopefully will not happen, such as dealing with an emergency.

For more detailed information about the options for assessment see Part Two: The assessment process – options for assessment.

ASSEMBLING AND STRUCTURING THE PORTFOLIO

Your portfolio needs some sort of structure and order. There are many ways to achieve this and we have listed below some that have proved to be most popular.

1. *Standards-based*

   The units and elements in the MCI standards can themselves be used as an organizational structure. Thus the portfolio would take the form:

Unit I	Element 1.1	Evidence:
Unit I	Element 1.2	Evidence:

   and so on.

   This has the advantage of being simple and universally accepted, and it also makes the mapping of the evidence onto the units and elements transparent.

   The disadvantage is that most people's jobs don't divide neatly into that format. There is also the issue of integration and repetition, whereby evidence produced to demonstrate competence in one element might also be evidence for others, and so on.

2. *Job description*

   The job itself can often be used as an organizing principle. Although many people have job descriptions that bear little relation to the work they do, there are those that are carefully constructed and can provide the basis for evidence. This is done by taking each component of the job description and collecting evidence for it.

3. *Project based*

   In this approach any projects, initiatives, procedures or anything that involves change in some way can generate evidence. Indeed, it is quite common for such projects to contain substantial evidence across all key role areas. What is important here is cross-referencing to the relevant units and elements.

4. *Other ways of assembling your portfolio*

   There are also an infinite number of organizational principles which will reflect the unique circumstances of your job, and you can be quite creative in the way that they are chosen. The following example might give you some ideas:

   Example A solicitor decided to track a customer's request from initial phone call right through negotiation, preparation of the brief, correspondence, court case and follow up. In other words she looked at her operation through the eyes of a customer and touched almost every aspect of her organization's work.

   If this might work for you then all well and good. Don't worry if you aren't yet in a position to make up your mind, it may be worth discussing with your manager and others which is the best approach to take.

Part Two: The assessment process

OVERVIEW OF THE PROCESS – WHAT SHOULD HAPPEN

The process for producing the portfolio usually follows this pattern:

1. For the key role area in question (e.g. Manage People), decide what evidence already exists to verify your competence in that area.

2. Compile a claim for competence describing how and why you have chosen to submit the evidence. This process is called 'storyboarding' and gives background information and context to your claims.

   Collect the evidence itself and compile a claim for competence. This should explain **why** the evidence is being submitted, the **background** to the issues or activities and how it meets the criteria.

3. You now need to decide how to provide evidence to meet the missing units and elements. This might be called a work-based activity and it is best to discuss this and agree with your mentor what form it might take.

   It might, for instance, be a personal account of some aspect of your work. Tracking a sale from initial query though to fulfillment would be a good example. It could also be a specific project or activity you could undertake in order to provide evidence. Some of the exercises contained in the Institute of Management Open Learning Programme workbooks could be used for this purpose.

Once you have agreed this with your mentor you should then complete a learning contract or agreement. You may wish to create your own format, but an example is set out below:

PRO FORMA LEARNING CONTRACT

Organizational information
Name:
Organization:
Programme:

Purpose of the activity

Description of the activity

Description of the likely evidence

Units/elements claimed

Start date_____   Finish date_____

FINDING AN ASSESSOR

Most of the Institute of Management approved centres listed in Section 8 of this guide can provide fully trained, professional assessors to support your development (however, note that not all of the centres provide NVQ assessment: some only offer certificate and diploma programmes and you should contact your nearest centre with details of your requirements).

In addition to an assessor you may also want the support of an APL adviser. This is a mentor with knowledge, skills and experience in this area. The adviser's role has three elements:

1. to help you, the candidate, to identify relevant achievements
2. to agree and review an action plan for achieving qualifications.
3. to help you to prepare and present evidence for assessment

It is useful to have the support of an adviser who can guide you through the assessment process, and most advisers are also assessors and know exactly what is required to provide a successful portfolio of evidence.

COLLECTING EVIDENCE

We now come to the collection of evidence itself. We shall take a 'top down' approach by looking at key roles, units and then elements. This may not fit exactly with the approach which you have decided to take (see Assembling and structuring the portfolio) but even if it is not, it is a good way of checking that your evidence provides coverage of the units and elements.

The methodology will be to use a simple algorithm, and then go to another level of detail with a set of questions as shown in Figure 2. These can either be used to generate evidence, or to check evidence for completion.

The following questions should act as a set of prompts to stimulate ideas. As they are related to units and elements, they will help you begin the process of mapping your own activities against the standards. In this way, they will act either as the first step of analysis against the algorithm above, or as the first stage of specification for your evidence.

Manage Activities

- What are the basic operational activities of my organization/division?
- If you are in a line function, it is likely that your operations relate to the business of the organization.
- If you are in a staff function the activities of your unit may well relate to one of the other key roles. For instance, if you are in personnel your activities may well be recruitment or staff development.

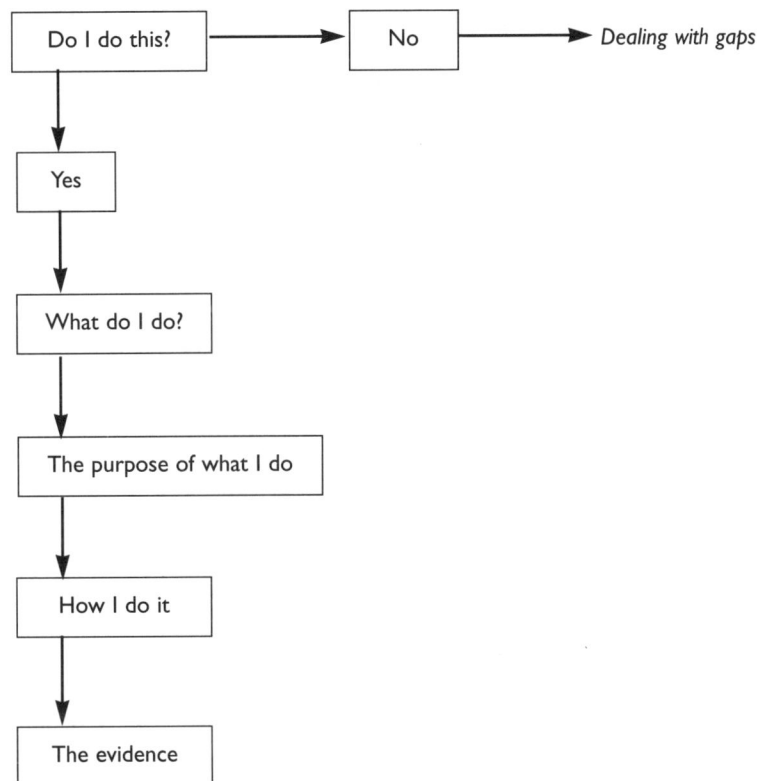

Figure 2 Flowchart for checking and collecting evidence

- If you are in finance your activities will be managing finance.
- If you are in information systems then your activities will be within managing information.
- In these cases, it should mean that the evidence for these two key roles will be the same.
- Who are your customers and what product or service do you supply to them?
- You might want to map your customers (internal and external) on a diagram.
- What standards are required of your unit, and how do you agree them?
- How do you organize the workspace and environment so that it is safe and conducive to productive work? Do you keep a health and safety record?
- What changes have you made (or should you make) to products, services, systems, activities, procedures? Why were these changes made, and how successful were they? What was your role in initiating these changes? How did you go about them?
- How is quality defined for your unit? How is it monitored?

Manage Resources

- Do you hold a budget or do you contribute to the budgeting process? What resources are you responsible for?

- For any changes you have proposed or been involved in, were the proposals costed and budgeted?
- How do you monitor the use of resources?

Manage People

In this section we concentrate on your team. It might be useful to set out who your team members are and what they do.

- Have you been involved in the recruitment and selection process?
- Have you made any assessment of future personnel requirements? Have you made recommendations for recruitment (or redundancy)?
- Have you advertised, shortlisted, interviewed or selected anyone for a job? If not, how would you go about it?
- What activities do you do collectively, as a team (e.g. meetings, briefings, working groups)?
- What have you done/do you do to develop individuals (appraisals, analysing training needs, delegating developmental tasks)?
- What are or have been your own development needs? What have you done to meet them?
- How do you allocate work to individuals within your team? How do you monitor it? How do you evaluate it, and how do you provide feedback? Do you use appraisals? What do you do when things go wrong or don't get done?
- How do you conduct your relationships with your:
  a) line manager
  b) peers or colleagues
  c) subordinates.
- How do you deal with conflicts, and how do you minimize potential conflicts? In what ways do you counsel staff, and with what results?

Manage Information

- What are the sources of information in your organization, division or unit? How is this information processed, stored, retrieved and used?
- How do you use information in consultation and discussion with others?
- What meetings do you lead, with what purposes and with what results?
- What reports do you prepare? Have you ever made a presentation to a group of individuals?

By answering these and related questions you will have collected ideas for a substantial body of evidence of your competence. Your written responses to these questions is in itself good evidence.

In order to transform and supplement this to make your evidence complete, there are a number of other considerations. One of these is the issue of ownership. Throughout your evidence you may make reference to documents, projects, initiatives, tasks and so on that are undertaken by your team. In each case it is necessary to separate out those aspects that you have responsibility for. In other words, we are asking the question

*What is **your** role and contribution to your unit of competence?*

It may be that this is obvious, or it may be spelt out in your account. In the latter case it is important to provide evidence to support your claims. **Testimonial evidence** is often a good way to do this.

The second issue is how often do we transform the answer to a simple question into complete evidence? There are many ways to do this. We will provide some short case studies to illustrate the possibilities.

CASE STUDY 1

James is a sales manager in a financial services organization. Ahead of the development of a company-wide scheme he has developed an appraisal scheme for his own department.

How can this be used to provide evidence?

First, he wrote an account of the appraisal scheme. In it he made reference to:

- why there was a need for the scheme
- the process by which he developed it – by consultation with line manager, subordinates, the personnel department
- the form and scope of the scheme
- how the scheme was implemented, including reference to a few particular examples
- a critical view of mistakes made and adjustments introduced
- a list of units and elements claimed by the evidence

This kind of personal account is an example of a storyboard. It might be a few pages or even shorter.

This was supported by a number of documents:

- minutes and notes of a tripartite meeting with his line manager and a representative of the personnel department
- the appraisal pro forma: draft and final versions
- two completed appraisal forms
- certificate of completion of a course in interviewing techniques for appraisal
- testimonials from his line manager and two of his subordinates attesting to the completion of the process

CASE STUDY 2

Marie is marketing manager in a service environment. She had the task of developing new advertising and promotional material for her organization's services. She produced a short (one page) storyboard about the tactical need for the project, and how she went about it. She added to this the following evidence:

- minutes of a departmental meeting at which she was tasked to undertake the project
- copies of the current material
- draft copies and the final version of the new material
- copies of correspondence and invoices from designers and printers
- a testimonial from her line manager appreciating the new material
- a copy of a letter from a customer in response to the new material
- costings presented to her line manager

CASE STUDY 3

Jean is a manager in the customer services section of a services organization. She developed a new customer inquiry monitoring system.

Jean wrote a short storyboard about why the system was necessary and how she went about developing it. This involved consulting with her subordinates who would be using the system.

Other evidence included:

- new and old customer enquiry forms
- an outline script for telephone enquiries
- graphs and bar charts analysing customer enquiries over a one-month period using the new system
- a short review of the outcomes and advantages of the new system (which included targets for individuals)

DEALING WITH GAPS IN EVIDENCE OR COMPETENCE

We have concentrated on those experiences and competences that you can demonstrate. But for almost everyone there is some part of the standards for which they find difficulty in showing competence or evidence of competence. For instance, some people have not been through a disciplinary or grievance procedure. Others have not been involved in developing a business strategy or plan.

What can we do in those circumstances? The first question to ask is:

Have I done this in previous employment?

If the answer is still no, you can then ask:

Have I done this, or something similar outside the work context?

If the answer is still no then a number of options can be tried.

One option is to show that you know and understand the correct procedure, and would be able to implement it in the necessary and appropriate circumstances. For instance, documenting the company disciplinary and grievance procedure, and giving a critical account of a real case (even if you were not involved) would demonstrate that you knew how to do it properly should the circumstances arise.

Another option would be to create for yourself an activity, such as a project or assignment within work, for the purposes of developing evidence. If this option is really necessary, it is best to agree it with your line manager, mentor and assessor in advance. This will help to make the project as 'natural' and as work-related as possible.

Other options that might work include:

- recording (or being observed in) role plays
- shadowing someone who performs that function

Once all of the evidence is collected it should be carefully organized. You might wish to use the following checklist:

1. Is the evidence organized and structured in a coherent and visible way?
2. Does the presentation make it easy to read and cross reference with the standards?
3. Are all of the elements of competence dealt with?
4. Is it obvious what each document is and why it is there?

MAPPING EVIDENCE TO THE ELEMENTS OF COMPETENCE

You now need to map your evidence to the units and elements of competence. This not only makes life easier for the assessor but it demonstrates your communication and information-handling skills.

If we were to just submit a huge collection of items (minutes, reports, memos and so forth) the assessor would be entitled to ask what the material was, and how it was organized. You need to indicate two things to the assessor:

1. how the material relates to the units and elements of competence
2. why it justifies your claim to competence in that element

This process is called **signposting** and without some system of signposting your evidence would be very confusing for the assessor.

There are many ways to do this, but one of the easiest is to produce a matrix. We list the discrete blocks of evidence (depending on our organizing principle) across the top, and the elements of competence down the side. We can then tick which elements we are claiming for which piece of evidence. Figure 3 illustrates an example matrix.

	Project A	Project B	Project C	Project D
Element 1.1	Strong evidence	Some evidence	Some evidence	
Element 1.2	Strong evidence		Some evidence	
Element 2.1				
Element 2.2	Strong evidence		Strong evidence	
Element 3.1		Strong evidence		
Element 3.2		Strong evidence		
Element 4.1				Strong evidence

Figure 3 An example matrix

It is quite likely that elements will have more than one piece of evidence against them. This is very good, as a single piece might imply that the evidence is weak.

PRESENTING PORTFOLIOS

Before presenting your portfolio for assessment you should make sure that it has the following components:

- title page
- contents – setting out your organizational approach
- a competence/contents map
- a job role audit form
- curriculum vitae
- job description

We can now move on to the process of assessment.

OPTIONS FOR ASSESSMENT

There are a wide range of options for assessment and formats for presenting information. They are by no means mutually exclusive, and some of the main options are explained below and include:

1. Assessment of Prior Learning (APL)
2. Observation; question and answer; intensive discussion with mentor
3. Assessment centre
4. Case study simulation
5. Work-based project; developmental activity
6. Reflective statement

Accreditation of Prior Learning (APL)

APL is a means of gaining accreditation for skills and achievements gained through past work experience. If you are seeking a management qualification then APL will almost certainly be important in helping you to achieve this, by recognizing your competence and achievements to date. Workbooks from the Institute of Management Open Learning Programme can then be used to supplement your skills and help develop your experience as a manager, ensuring that you are not repeating anything which you may already have learnt from experience.

Past and current experience The following is a quick checklist which should help you to determine whether the APL process is suitable for you. You should be able to answer yes to all or most of the following questions:

- Do I have experience of employment, including management responsibility?
- Have I been involved in a variety of management tasks and responsibilities?
- Have I been responsible for the work of other people?
- Have I been responsible for resources – particularly financial resources?
- Have I had an impact or influence on a product or service?

Personal requirements If you can answer yes to all or most of the following questions, you are likely to be able to achieve success in the APL process:

- Do I have some time over the next few months to devote to this?
- Am I willing to examine and assess my own experience and capability?
- Do I have a creative and flexible approach to solving problems?
- Do I have access to the support and help of others – both at home and at work?
- Do I have written communication skills?

These questions are not only valid if you are considering starting the APL process, but are also relevant before you contemplate starting to study the Institute of Management Open Learning Programme. The workbooks, activities and exercises in the series will provide both stimulation and a considerable challenge!

Mentoring Experience has shown that the support of other people, mentors, can make a substantial difference and be a great source of help to people involved in any process of assessment and self-development. Mentors can offer assistance in the following ways:

1. they have management experience and can explain management ideas and practice
2. they can help you to apply your skills, whether recently learnt or not, to your actual situation at work
3. they have knowledge of the national standards and the assessment process
4. they can advise and coach you
5. they have time to devote to you
6. they support self-development
7. they are good problem solvers
8. they can help provide a valuable perspective on a particular situation and provide an objective opinion
9. they provide an informed sounding board for your opinions
10. they know how to give feedback
11. they can counsel and motivate you

It may well be that you will need, or want to have, more than one person to satisfy all of these needs. For instance, the counsellor and the expert could well be different people.

MENTORING ACTIVITY

Look at the list above and identify one or more people who can support and mentor you through this process. Specify which of your needs they can satisfy.

The next step is to negotiate with each mentor on your list about the nature of their involvement and commitment. The negotiation often results in a learning contract or agreement. Like all agreements, it should be two way. You should define:

- what you intend to do
- what resources you will need
- signposts or stages of achievement

You can then agree with your mentor:

- what their contribution will be
- the time(s) they are willing to devote
- the status and confidentiality elements of the relationship

APL: Action checklist

1. *Get some good initial advice*

   This is probably the most important stage. APL sounds very attractive because it seems to offer a fast track to qualifications without any effort. In reality, it involves a lot of work and only suits certain people. That is why it is important that you approach a provider with considerable expertise in this area. Make sure you get clear answers to the following questions:
   - the relative costs of APL compared to other routes
   - the possibility of embedding the programme within normal company processes
   - the likely timespan and probability of success (success rates can be as low as five per cent – ask any training provider you are talking to!).

2. *Review previous experience against the national standards*

   Again, the quality of the advice you receive at the start of a programme will affect the speed and ease through the APL process. Once you have decided to embark on the APL process, effective providers will usually provide a variety of profiling devices to measure your previous experience, along with valuable counselling on the level of qualification to be sought and the best way to go about it. At the end of this stage you should have received:
   - an explanation of all the options available
   - a review of your experience (i.e. mapping) against the national standards and advice on the appropriate level
   - identification of shortfalls in experience and suggestions as to what to do about these
   - an induction programme explaining the nature of standards and how to accumulate evidence
   - help and guidance if you have special needs
   - a counsellor or adviser allocated to you.

3. *Draw up an action plan*

   Once you have some idea of how your experience maps on to the standards or criteria that you will be assessed against, you will need to start planning how you are going to accumulate the evidence. Some centres like to provide additional seminars or self-help groups (action learning sets) to support the planning process.

Finally, the evidence needs to be presented clearly by providing summary descriptions (often called storyboards) and summary lists of evidence, explaining their significance and how they map to the elements of competence.

4. *Submit the evidence for assessment*

    Arrangements will vary between centres, but normally the portfolio will be sent to an assessor who will assess the evidence within a few weeks and then arrange an interview to clarify details. At the end of the interview the assessor will identify the units and elements of competence which have been accepted. If some of the evidence has not been accepted, the assessor will identify what evidence will need to be produced to satisfy the national standards and probably discuss ways of gaining the necessary evidence.

A few thought starters if you are considering APL

1. Although you may be confident in your abilities, think how you would convince someone from another industry or business of your competence if you were forced to change jobs. Is APL an option?
2. Another way of looking at APL is to see it as a form of quality accreditation designed for the individual. It takes guts to put yourself on the line and have a stranger assess everything you do.

A few dos and don'ts for APL

Do

■ Make sure that you get advice from someone with plenty of experience in running APL programmes. Assessors should be qualified and should have the special TDLB (Training and Development Lead Body) units for assessors.
■ Ask the centre to put you in touch with people who have completed the APL process.
■ Ensure that counsellors or advisers at the centre are experienced managers who understand your business.
■ Consider embedding an APL programme in initiatives within the company, such as quality initiative, change programmes or special projects.
■ Develop support mechanisms within the company to promote learning and assist APL candidates.

Don't

■ Rush into APL simply because it sounds like a good idea and someone has provided the money for it.
■ Go for the cheapest option. APL is no less expensive than other traditional programmes.
■ Imagine that it is going to be an easy alternative to traditional methods of gaining qualifications.

- Assume that you are competent in all areas just because you are an experienced manager. APL often highlights certain gaps in experience which may require further development.
- Walk away from the process once started!

Observation

This evidence would normally take the form of notes by the assessor that a given activity had been observed; the circumstances in which it was carried out, and the extent to which competence was demonstrated. Observation is not only of an activity. It can also include evaluating workplace settings which a candidate has responsibility for. It is important that the assessor's notes and comments are included in the portfolio.

Assessment centre

An assessment centre consists of a carefully designed programme of job-related simulation exercises, in which the performance of a group of participants is observed and evaluated by the assessor. Development centres are similar in design and structure, but have a very different purpose. Because they are designed to help participants to learn more about themselves, development centres generally provide much more feedback from assessors.

Case study simulation

Case studies and role plays can be very useful in generating evidence for events which might not normally occur: for example, a disciplinary interview or an emergency in the workplace. They are also useful for those activities where you simply do not have the opportunity to use or prove the skills that you possess: for example, you may be an excellent mentor but be without any evidence, past or present, of your success. In these circumstances a role play observed by the assessor can be very useful, and it is in many ways similar to the type of activity carried out at an assessment centre.

The only note of caution is to remember the purpose of the exercise, and not to overact! Remember to be natural, treating the situation as if it were nothing less than reality.

Work-based project and developmental activity

A work-based activity is frequently the most practical, beneficial form of evidence. While much evidence collection can be a historical, retrospective exercise, work-based activity take the skills and techniques learnt in the workbooks or as a result of experience, and applies them in order to initiate change and improvements. One of the strengths of the Institute of Management Open Learning Programme's workbooks is their focus on practical, continuous improvement, and activities which stimulate and encourage work-based projects.

As a source of evidence for your portfolio and assessor they can provide a rich variety of management skills and cover a wide range of elements, although choosing the right project is obviously essential. It is worth bearing in mind that your work-based project or activity should be SMART, and it is certainly worth discussing with your manager and mentor what would be the best project to undertake.

The final check

One function that mentors should perform well is a pre-assessment. Although they may not be assessors themselves they can give a gut feel response. If your evidence convinces them it is quite likely to convince an assessor.

It is worth remembering that most candidates do not prepare a complete portfolio before submitting evidence to an assessor. Be prepared to enter into a dialogue with the assessor, to discuss ideas and to submit evidence bit by bit. In this way you will get to understand what the assessor needs from you, and how you can best meet the standards.

Assessor's criteria

You should know the basis on which the assessor will assess your evidence. The following list of the criteria that are used provide a useful test for your own evidence.

- *Currency* – is the evidence recent enough to show current best practice? This is a quality/quantity issue. In general, the further we need to go back the less valid is the experience. If most of our evidence is over five years old this might be considered quite weak. Up to one year is always acceptable.
- *Authenticity* – how can you show that this evidence relates to your own performance? Can you separate out your contribution?
- *Sufficiency* – is there enough evidence to demonstrate competence? Again, this is a quality/quantity issue. For instance, if you counsel staff regularly then one documented case might be sufficient. On the other hand, if your only experience was in a simulation then a single instance would be unlikely to be sufficient.

- *Validity* – does the evidence relate to the competence in question? If you were to present evidence that your department had zero staff turnover in the last year, it might be good evidence. However, it might not show that you counsel your staff competently. (As a matter of interest, what do you think it might demonstrate?)

You should also bear in mind that this style and approach to assessment is quite different to more traditional styles of 'terminal' assessment and examination.

One of the most important implications of this is the notion of **dialogue** with the assessor. The assessor needs to know something about your work environment. There are a number of ways that the assessor can obtain this:

1. *The job role audit form* – or some other form of personal account
2. *Discussion* – meeting with the assessor who can then ask questions
3. *Directly* – the assessor can visit your workplace and even observe you at work

Whichever combination of these is most appropriate is to be decided jointly between you and the assessor. What is vital is that this kind of dialogue begins early in the process.

Another benefit of this dialogue is that it enables constructive feedback to take place. Whether this feedback concerns your competence directly, or your ideas about evidence, it will enable you to understand the requirements of the assessor.

Finally, a word about confidentiality. There may be cases where the nature of your evidence makes it sensitive – either from the personal or commercial point of view. Can this cause a problem? The short answer is that it shouldn't.

The contract of assessment is between you and the assessor, and they have a strict duty of confidentiality. The material you submit may not be circulated or published without your express permission. In fact, neither will it be photocopied as it remains your property.

If, even on this basis, there is still a problem, here are a few possible approaches:

- if names of individuals are on documents – they should be removed or obscured
- if documents contain confidential figures (e.g. in budgets), the actual figures could be erased. They could also all be multiplied by a random number known only to you (in these circumstances you will need to inform the assessor of what you had done)
- if these documents are not sufficient, then the sensitive documents can be shown to the assessor 'sight only' in the workplace

Section 8 Further information

This section includes details of:

- useful further reading
- useful addresses
- centres approved to run Institute of Management programmes and to award qualifications

Useful further reading

Personal Effectiveness
Alexander Murdock and Carol Scutt, Butterworth-Heinemann/Institute of Management, Oxford, 1993

Open Learning Choices for Managers – a guide for buyers
Prometheus Consulting, Wokingham

NVQ Handbook – practical guidelines for providers and assessors
John Walton, Butterworth-Heinemann/Institute of Management, Oxford, 1996

Successful Training in a Week
Malcolm Peel, Hodder Headline, London, 1995

Resource-Based Learning
Julie Dorrell, McGraw-Hill, Maidenhead, 1993

For further information and addresses, including details of books and articles on all aspects of management training and development, contact the Management Information Centre at the Institute of Management.

Useful addresses

Institute of Management
Management House
Cottingham Road
Corby
Northamptonshire NN17 1TT
Tel: 01536 204222
Fax: 01536 201651

Pergamon Open Learning (publishers of the Management Development
Programme)
Butterworth-Heinemann
Linacre House
Jordan Hill
Oxford OX2 8DP
Tel: 01865 310366
Fax: 01865 310898

Other organizations which provide qualifications in management include:

BTEC/Edexcel
Central House
Upper Woburn Place
London WC1H 0HH
Tel: 0171 413 8400
Fax: 0171 387 6068

City and Guilds of London Institute
1 Giltspur Street
London EC1A 9DD
Tel: 0171 294 2468
Fax: 0171 294 2400

Henley Management College
Greenlands
Henley-on-Thames
Oxfordshire RG9 3AU
Tel: 01491 571454
Fax: 01491 571635

Institute of Personnel and Development
IPD House
35 Camp Road
Wimbledon
London SW19 4UX
Tel: 0181 971 9000
Fax: 0181 947 2570

London Chamber of Commerce and Industry Examinations Board
Marlowe House
Station Road
Sidcup
Kent DA15 7BJ
Tel: 0181 302 0261
Fax: 0181 302 4169/5169

NEBS Management
1 Giltspur Street
London EC1A 9DD
Tel: 0171 294 2470
Fax: 0171 294 2402

RSA Examination Board
Westwood Way
Coventry CV4 8HS
Tel: 01203 470033
Fax: 01203 468080

The following are the main accrediting bodies for NVQs:

National Council for Vocational Qualifications (NCVQ)
222 Euston Road
London NW1 2BZ
Tel: 0171 387 9898
Fax: 0171 387 0978

Scottish Qualifications Authority (SQA)
Hanover House
24 Douglas Street
Glasgow G2 7NQ
Tel: 0141 248 7900
Fax: 0141 242 2244

Training and Enterprise Councils – Local Enterprise Councils in Scotland –
provide help and advice on training to enable you to identify what will be best
to suit your needs. For further information, contact your local TEC or LEC, or:

For TECs
Tel: 01142 594776
Fax: 01142 593359

For LECs
Tel: 0141 248 2700
Fax: 0141 228 2511

Business Links

Business Links – formed by local partnerships of business support organizations to give one-stop access to a full range of services – have been opened throughout England. To contact your local business link contact the DTI, your local TEC or Chamber of Commerce, or call 01142 597507/8.

Centres approved to run Institute of Management programmes and to award qualifications

The following centres have been approved by the Institute of Management to run management development programmes at Certificate, Diploma and S/NVQ Levels 4 and 5.

ENGLAND – NORTH WEST

Bury College
Whitefield Centre
Albert Road
Whitefield
Manchester M25 6NH
Mr. G Cleary
Tel. 0161 7632524

Carlisle College
Victoria Place
Carlisle
Cumbria CA1 1HS
Ms R Illingworth
Tel. 01228 24464

City College Manchester
Fielden Centre
141 Barlow Moor Road
West Didsbury
Manchester M20 2PQ
Mr. G Gobbett
Tel. 0161 957 1610

City of Liverpool Community College
Aulis House
Riversdale Road
Liverpool L19 3QN
Ms L Hindley
Tel. 0151 252 4825/6

Company Plus Ltd
Padgate Campus
Fearnhead Lane
Fearnhead
Warrington WA2 0NY
Mrs. C Blades
Tel. 01925 824082

Furness College
Howard Street
Barrow in Furness
Cumbria LA 14 1LU
Mr. S Lever
Tel. 01229 825017

Lancaster and Morecambe College of Further Education
Morecambe Road
Lancaster LA1 2TY
Mr. D Bennett
Tel. 01524 66215

Stockport College of Further and Higher Education
The Davenport Centre
Highfield Close
Stockport SK3 8UA
Mr. R Hall
Tel. 0161 958 3605

The Development Partnership
Victoria House
9 Rivington Avenue
Wincile City
St. Helens
Merseyside
Ms J Barton
Tel. 01744 602563
(note: not approved at NVQ level 5)

The Open College
St. Pauls
781 Wilmslow Road
Didsbury
Manchester M20 2RW
Ms J Rhodes
Tel. 0161 434 0007

The Summit Management Centre
The Ridge College
Hibbert Lane
Marple
Stockport SK6 7PA
Ms Janet Milligan
Tel. 0161 4277733

University College Salford
Dept. of Management Studies
Frederick Road
Salford
Lancashire M6 6PU
Tel. 0161 736 6541

West Cumbria College
Park Lane
Workington
Cumbria CA14 2 RW
Mrs. E Beck
Tel. 01900 64331

Wigan and Leigh College
Room 350
Page Field Building
Bridgeman Terrace
Wigan
Lancashire WN1 1TX
Mr. D Harrison
Tel. 01942 501885/6

Wirral Metropolitan College
International Business and Management Centre
Europa Boulevard
Conway Park
Birkenhead
Wirral L41 4NT
Mr. D Moulton
Tel. 0151 6493000

ENGLAND – NORTH EAST

Bradford Training Association
BTAL House
Laisterdyke
Bradford BD4 8AT
Mr. K MacKenzie
Tel. 01274 668149

Darlington College of Technology
Management and Professional Studies Centre
Chesterfield
64 – 66 Stanhope Road
Darlington
Co. Durham DL3 7SE
Mrs. P Hall
Tel. 01325 503050

Dearne Valley Business School
Doncaster College
Barnsley Road
High Melton
Doncaster DN5 7SZ
Mr. G Pell
Tel. 01302 553553

Durham University Business School
Small Business Centre
Mill Hill Lane
Durham City
DH1 3LB
Mr. B Snaith
Tel. 0191 374 2211

Gateshead College
Durham Road
Gateshead
Tyne and Wear
NE9 5BN
Mr. G Spencer
Tel. 0191 4902263

Harrogate College
Hornbeam Park
Harrogate HG2 8QT
Mr. P Dix
Tel. 01423 878299
(note: not approved at NVQ level 5)

Hull College
Queens Gardens
Hull HU1 3DG
Ms H Rainey
Tel. 01482 329943

Newcastle Business School
University of Northumbria at Newcastle
Flexible Learning Centre, Room 239
Northumberland Building
Northumberland Road
Newcastle upon Tyne NE1 8ST
Mr. S Hall
Tel. 0191 227 3837

New College Durham
Faculty of Administration and Business
Nevilles Cross Centre
Durham
Co Durham DH1 4SY
Mr. P McLoughlin
Tel. 0191 384 7325

North Nottinghamshire College of Further Education
Department of Management Studies
Carlton Road
Worksop
Nottinghamshire S81 7HP
Mr. J Hill
Tel. 01909 473561

Project North East
Design Works
William Street
Felling
Gateshead NE10 0JP
Ms. T Etherington
Tel. 0191 495 0066
(note: not approved at NVQ level 5)

Selby College
Abbots Road
Selby
North Yorkshire YO8 8AT
Mr. B Crosson
Tel. 01757 211000
(note: not approved at NVQ level 5)

South Tyneside College
St. Georges Avenue
South Shields
Tyne and Wear NE34 6ET
Mr. W G Maw
Tel. 0191 427 3500

Springfield Management Ltd
Anchor House
The Maltings
Hull HU1 3HA
Mr. N Bardsley
Tel. 01482 221356

Stockton and Billingham College
Department of Business
Oxbridge Avenue
Stockton
Cleveland TS18 4QA
Mr. D Eggleston
Tel. 01642 672317

TTA (North)
Micklewood House
Longhirst Hall
Longhirst
Morpeth
Northumberland NE61 3LL
Mr. J Fatherly
Tel. 01670 795161

The Learning Exchange
Marvell House
Cranbourne House
Hull HU3 1PQ
Ms. H Kitchen
Tel. 01482 211918
(note: not approved at NVQ level 5)

The Sheffield College
School of Management Development
Parson Cross Centre
Remington Road
Sheffield S5 9PB
Mr. P E Lester
Tel. 0114 260 2500

University of York
Centre for Continuing Education
Heslington
York YO1 5DD
Mrs. S Vassie
Tel. 01904 434622

Wakefield College
School of Management and Professional Studies
Thornes Park
Wakefield WF2 8QZ
Mr. T Biscomb
Tel. 01924 789828/9

York College of Further and Higher Education
Tadcaster Road
York YO2 1UQ
Ms. K Christie
Tel. 01904 770354

York Computing and Management Centre
First Floor
21 New Street
York YO1 2RA
Mr. D Bell
Tel. 01904 672656

ENGLAND – EAST MIDLANDS

Burton-upon-Trent Technical College
Forest Business Centre
Station Road
Rolleston-on-Dove
Staffordshire DE13 9AB
Ms C Jones
Tel: 01283 812333

Institute of Management
Competent Manager Programme
Management House
Cottingham Road
Corby
Northamptonshire NN17 1TT
Mrs J Morton
Tel: 01536 204222

Newark and Sherwood College
Friary Road
Newark
Nottinghamshire NG24 1PB
Mr Z Zamo
Tel: 01636 680680

Tamworth College of Further Education
Croft Street
Upper Gungate
Tamworth
Staffordshire B79 8AE
Mr G Cooper
Tel: 01827 310202
(note: not approved at NVQ Level 5)

University of Derby
Kedleston Road
Derby DE3 1GB
Mr P Hollingshead
Tel: 01332 347181 Ext. 1862

ENGLAND – EAST ANGLIA

Cambridge HSSM
Training and Development Services
Chesterton Hospital
Union Lane
Cambridge CB4 1PT
Mr A Rance
Tel: 01223 884000
(note: not approved at NVQ Level 4)

Cambridge Regional College
King Hedges Road
Cambridge CB4 2QT
Ms J Robertson
Tel: 01223 418200

Colchester Institute
Sheepen Road
Colchester
Essex CO3 3LL
Mr D Roberts
Tel: 01206 718122

Huntingdonshire Regional College
Department of Business and Management
California Road
Huntingdon PE18 7BL
Ms L Stannard
Tel: 01480 52346

North Lincolnshire College
Lincoln Centre
Monks Road
Lincoln
Lincolnshire LN2 5HQ
Mr M Wood
Tel: 01522 510530

Peterborough Regional College
Centre of Financial and Management Studies
Forward House
Shrovesbury Avenue
Peterborough PE2 6BX
Mr R Barnard
Tel: 01733 370582

ENGLAND – GREATER LONDON

Barking College
Dagenham Road
Romford
Essex RM7 0XU
Ms Y Richardson
Tel: 01708 766841
(note: not approved at NVQ Level 5)

Bexley College
School of Business, Leisure and Tourism
Tower Road
Belvedere
Kent DA17 6JA
Mr P Rae
Tel: 01322 442331

Bromley College of Further and Higher Education
Rookery Lane
Bromley
Kent BR2 8HE
Mr K Vincent
Tel: 0181 295 7000

City of Westminster College
Training Services – Room 4
Lancaster Road
Ladbroke Grove
London W11 1QT
Ms I Duvigneau
Tel: 0171 258 2961/2/3/4/5/6

Surrey YACES
Education Centre
The Runnymede Centre
Chertsey Road
Addlestone
Surrey KT15 2EP
Mr C Norris
Tel: 01932 570946

(note: not approved at NVQ Level 5)

Training Services Management Development Centre
Ladbroke Grove Centre
Lancaster Road
London W11 1QT
Mr P Tudor
Tel: 0171 258 2961

University of East London
Post Experience Studies
Duncan House
High Street
London E15 2JB
Mr M Rowswell
Tel: 0181 590 7722

ENGLAND – NORTHERN HOME COUNTIES

Bedford College
Cauldwell Street
Bedford MK42 9AH
Ms K Harper
Tel: 01234 345151
(note: not approved at NVQ Level 5)

Harlow College
Commercial Services Ltd
College Square
The High
Harlow
Essex CM20 1LT
Ms M Abbott
Tel: 01279 868200

Southend Enterprise Agency Ltd
Enterprise House
853-855 London Road
Westcliff-on-Sea
Essex SS0 9ST
Mr T McCormack
Tel: 01702 471118

West Hertfordshire Management Centre
Bucks Hill House
Nr Chipperfield
Kings Langley
Hertfordshire WD4 9AP
Mr P Boggon
Tel: 01923 262622

Bilston Community College
Green Lanes Campus
Wellington Road
Bilston
West Midlands WV14 6EW
Mr P Harrison
Tel: 01902 408791

CMTC Management Centre
Woodland Grange
Old Milverton Lane
Leamington Spa
Warwickshire CV32 6RN
Mr G Platt
Tel: 01926 336621

Corporate Training and Development Ltd
Keric House West
197 Hagley Road
Edgbaston
Birmingham B16 9RD
Ms D Williams
Tel: 0121 454 5553
(note: not approved at NVQ Level 5)

Dudley College of Technology
The Broadway
Dudley
West Midlands DY1 4AS
Mr A Dennant
Tel: 01384 455433

Dunchurch Executive Accreditation Centre
GEC Management College
Dunchurch
Rugby
Warwickshire CV22 6QW
Mr P Kyne
Tel: 01788 810656 Ext. 2054

Hawk Management Services
The Management Centre
King Street
Newcastle-under-Lyme
Staffordshire ST5 1EN
Mr R Moore
Tel: 01782 715522

Herefordshire College of Technology
Hereford Education and Conference Centre
Blackfriars Street
Hereford HR4 9HS
Mr W Hill
Tel: 01432 352235

INTEC Business Colleges
2 Market Place
Rugby
Warwickshire CV21 3DY
Mr J Moore
Tel: 01788 575090
(note: not approved at NVQ Level 5)

Warwickshire College
Royal Leamington Spa and Moreton Morrell
Department of Business Studies
Warwick New Road
Leamington
Warwickshire CV32 5JE
Mr M Pelling
Tel: 01926 311711

Most Management Training Ltd
Bloomfield Road
Tipton
West Midlands DY4 9AH
Mr B Callard
Tel: 0121 557 3280

North East Worcestershire College
Department of Management Studies
Blackwood Road
Bromsgrove
Worcestershire B60 1BB
Mr D Lewis
Tel: 01527 570020

North Warwickshire and Hinckley College
Hinckley Road
Nuneaton
Warwickshire CV11 6BH
Mr C Salter
Tel: 01203 349321

Sandwell College of Further and Higher Education
Wednesbury Campus
Woden Road South
Wednesbury
Sandwell
West Midlands WS10 0PE
Mr D Proud
Tel: 0121 556 6000

Solihull College
Management Division
Blossomfield Road
Solihull
West Midlands B91 1SB
Mr MA Gibson
Tel: 0121 711 2111

Staffordshire University
Leek Road
Stoke-on-Trent
Staffordshire ST4 2DE
Mr K Moreton
Tel: 01782 412515

Sutton Management Centre
Department of Business Studies
Lichfield Road
Sutton Coldfield
West Midlands B74 2NW
Mr W Carter
Tel: 0121 355 5671

Telford College of Art and Technology
Walker Annexe
Hartsbridge Road
Oakengates
Telford TF2 6BA
Mr G Cryer
Tel: 01952 620195

Telford Management Services
The Cedars
39-41 Compton Road West
Wolverhampton WV3 9DW
Mr A Haywood
Tel: 01902 20999
(note: not approved at NVQ Level 5)

Walsall College of Technology
St. Pauls Street
Walsall
West Midlands WS1 1XN
Mr EC Bailey
Tel: 01922 657000

Worcester Technical College
Department of Business Studies
Victoria Annexe
Samson Walk
Worcester WR1 1PQ
Mr D Portsmouth
Tel: 01905 723383

ENGLAND – SOUTH EAST

Canterbury College
New Dover Road
Canterbury
Kent CT1 3AJ
Mr G Metcalfe
Tel: 01227 766081
(note: not approved at NVQ Level 5)

South Kent College
Maison Dieu Road
Dover
Kent CT16 1DH
Mr R Dean
Tel: 01304 204573

The University of Brighton Business School
The Centre for Management Development
Mithras House
Lewes Road
Brighton
East Sussex BN2 4AT
Mr J Lawson
Tel: 01273 600900

ENGLAND – SOUTH WEST

College of Further Education Plymouth
Plymouth Management and Business Centre
Floor 6
Kings Road
Devonport
Plymouth P11 5QG
Ms V Miller
Tel: 01752 385392

Cornwall College
Trevenson House
Redruth
Cornwall TR15 3RD
Mr J Newman
Tel: 01209 712911/612828

North Devon College
Department of Business Studies
Old Sticklepath Hill
Barnstaple
Devon EX31 2BQ
Mr RK Bryan
Tel: 01271 45291

Strode College
Business and Secretarial Department
Church Road
Street
Somerset BA16 0AB
Mr PS Davies
Tel: 01458 844400
(note: not approved at NVQ Level 5)

Yeovil College
Holland Campus
Mudford Road
Yeovil
Somerset BA21 4DR
Mr D Lee
Tel: 01935 23921

ENGLAND – SOUTHERN COUNTIES

Basingstoke College of Technology
Management Centre
John Hunt of Everest
School Campus
Popley Way
Basingstoke RG21 9AB
Ms A Symons
Tel: 01256 64477

Bournemouth and Poole College
Supervisory Management Unit
North Road
Parkstone
Poole BH14 0LS
Mr J Nimmo
Tel: 01202 747600

Chichester College
Department of Management and Business Studies
Westgate Fields
Chichester
West Sussex PO19 1SB
Ms J Allebone
Tel: 01234 786321

Grosvenor Training Services
Stanford House
South Road
Brighton BN1 6SB
Mr C Cox
Tel: 01273 566261

Highlands College
Management Centre
PO Box 1000
St. Saviour
Jersey JE4 9QA
Ms A Watkins
Tel: 01534 58289

Isle of Wight College of Art and Technology
Medina Way
Newport
Isle of Wight PO30 5TA
Mr M Barrett
Tel: 01983 526631

North Hampshire Business School
Farnborough College
Boundary Road
Farnborough
Hampshire GU14 6SB
Mr B Kemp
Tel: 01252 515511

Salisbury College Management Centre
Southampton Road
Salisbury
Wiltshire SP1 2LW
Mr D Knapp
Tel: 01722 323711

South Downs College
College Road
Havant
Hampshire PO7 8AA
Mr H Denny
Tel: 01705 797979

Southampton City College
St. Mary Street
Southampton SO9 4WX
Ms I Chapman
Tel: 01703 635222

ENGLAND – WEST

City of Bath College
School of Business and Management
Avon Street
Bath
Avon BA1 1UP
Ms S Leahy
Tel: 01225 312191

Cygnet Business Development
Noggins
35 Lower Radley
Abingdon
Oxfordshire OX14 3AY
Mr J Coleman
Tel: 01235 535786

Gayton Consultancy and Training
12 Pierrepont Street
Bath BA1 1LA
Ms U Neil
Tel: 01225 448656
(note: not approved at NVQ Level 5)

New College Swindon
Helston Road
Park North
Swindon SN3 2LA
Mr A Williams
Tel: 01793 611470

South Bristol College
Business Development Training
Old Custom House
Queen Square
Bristol BS1 4JH
Mr R Slocombe
Tel: 0117 929 1680

Stroud College
Department of Business and Management Studies
Stratford Road
Stroud
Gloucestershire GL5 4AH
Mr D Carter
Tel: 01453 763424

The Guide Dogs for the Blind
Hillfields
Burghfields
Reading RG7 3YG
Ms AT Oberon
Tel: 01734 835555
(note: not approved at NVQ Level 5)

The Management Centre
Management Centre
London Road
Warmley
Bristol BS15 5JH
Mr S Isherwood
Tel: 0117 967 7807

Wiltshire Management Centre
Swindon College
Regent Circus
Swindon SN1 1PT
Mr R Paris
Tel: 01793 498387

NORTHERN IRELAND

Belfast Institute of Further and Higher Education
College Square East
Belfast
Northern Ireland BT1 6DJ
Mr P Baxter
Tel: 01232 265000

Gwen Savage & Co Ltd
69 High Street
Bangor
Co. Down
Northern Ireland BT20 5BD
Mr I Savage
Tel: 01247 461122
(note: not approved at NVQ level 5)

Newry Technical College
Patrick Street
Newry
Co. Down
Northern Ireland
Mr JB Lannon
Tel: 01693 61071

North Down and Ards College of Further Education
Castle Park Road
Bangor
Co. Down
Northern Ireland BT20 4TF
Mrs H Holmes
Tel: 01247 271254

North West Institute of Further and Higher Education
Department of Business and Management Studies
Strand Road
Londonderry
Northern Ireland BY48 7BY
Ms P Gormley
Tel: 01504 266711
(note: not approved at NVQ Level 5)

Parity Solutions (Ireland) Ltd
Blackstaff Chambers
2 Amelia Street
Belfast
Northern Ireland BT2 7GS
Mr S Wallace
Tel: 01232 240780
(note: not approved at NVQ Level 5)

SCOTLAND

Ayr College
Department of Business and Management
Dam Park
Ayr
Ayrshire KA8 0EU
Mr P Padden
Tel: 01292 265184

BCG
3/5 High Street
Paisley
Renfrewshire PA1 2AE
Mr GH Marshall
Tel: 0141 849 1400

Clydebank College
Department of Technology and Administration
Kilbowie Road
Clydebank
Dunbartonshire G81 2AA
Mr G Lyon
Tel: 0141 952 7771

Fife College of Further and Higher Education
Department of Management and Professional Studies
St Brycedale Avenue
Kirkcaldy
Fife KY1 1EX
Mr G Miller
Tel: 01592 268591

The Training Partnership
Cairngorm Development Ltd
87 St Vincent Street
Glasgow G2 5TF
Ms S McHenry
Tel: 0141 221 2557

WALES

Gwent Tertiary College
Ebbw Vale Campus
College Road
Ebbw Vale
Gwent NP3 6LE
Mr T Griffiths
Tel: 01495 302083

Infinet
University of Wales Bangor
58 Maesog College Road
Bangor
Gwynedd LL57 2DG
Ms G Rankin
Tel: 01248 382644

MADE
The Gadleys
Aberdare
Mid Glamorgan CF44 8DL
Mr JA Jones
Tel: 01685 882515

Myrick Training Services
Myrick House
Hendomen
Montgomery
Powys SY15 6EZ
Mr C Cave
Tel: 01686 668670

Swansea College
Tycoch Road
Swansea
West Glamorgan SA2 9EB
Ms C Whyte
Tel: 01792 284000

The Chrysalis Group
Lulworth House
Monk Street
Abergavenny
Gwent NP7 5NP
Mr J Taylor
Tel: 01873 857070

Ystrad Mynach College
Twyn Road
Hengoed
Mid Glamorgan CF7 8XR
Ms M Thomas
Tel: 01443 816888
(Note: this information is correct at time of going to print.)

About the Institute of Management

The mission of the Institute of Management (IM) is to promote the development, exercise and recognition of professional management.

The IM is the leading professional organization for managers. Its efforts and resources are devoted to ensuring the continuing development and success of its members.

At the forefront of management standards, the IM provides a range of services for its members. These include flexible training programmes and a unique range of support services such as career counselling, enquiry and research facilities and preferential prices on IM publications and other IM products.

Further details about the Institute of Management may be obtained from:

Institute of Management
Management House
Cottingham Road
Corby
Northants
NN17 1TT

Telephone 01536 204222